Communion
Outside
the Eucharist

by Phillip Tovey

Team Vicar, Banbury

THE ALCUIN CLUB and the GROUP FOR RENEWAL OF WORSHIP (GROW)

The Alcuin Club, which exists to promote the study of Christian liturgy in general and of Anglican liturgy in particular, traditionally published a single volume annually for its members. This ceased in 1986 but resumed in 1992. Similarly, GROW was responsible from 1975 to 1986 for the quarterly 'Grove Liturgical Studies'. Since the beginning of 1987 the two have sponsored a Joint Editorial Board to produce quarterly 'Joint Liturgical Studies', details of which are to be found at the end of this Study.

THE COVER PICTURE

Shows: the Rev. Graham Woolfenden officiating at the Liturgy of the Presanctified; the Rev. Maureen Turner officiating at extended Communion at Holy Trinity Church, Stratford-on-Avon; Mrs. Bernadette Studdard at a training session for lay presiders for eucharistic services in the absence of a priest.

First Impression December 1993
ISSN 0951-2667
ISBN 1 85174 255 7

GROVE BOOKS LIMITED
Bramcote   Nottingham   NG9 3DS

CONTENTS

ACKNOWLEDGMENTS

The author and publishers acknowledge with thanks permission to reproduce copyright material in chapter 9 as follows:

Texts 1 and 2: from *Sunday Celebration*, copyright International Committee for English in the Liturgy (ICEL).

Texts 3, 4 and 7: no copyright is claimed.

Texts 5 and 6: out of copyright.

Texts 8 and 9: from *A New Zealand Prayer Book*, copyright Church of the Province of New Zealand.

Text 10: no copyright is claimed for this as a publication, but permission to reproduce it has been given by the Archbishop of Wales.

Texts 11 and 12: from *Communion*, copyright the General Synod of the Scottish Episcopal Church.

Texts 13 and 14: the former of these is adapted from the ASB and the latter is reproduced from *Ministry to the Sick*, both copyright the Central Board of Finance of the Church of England.

1. Introduction

There has been, from time to time in the history of the church, the provision of communion outside the eucharist. This has been in a number of contexts, domestic, monastic, and parish. It has taken a variety of liturgical forms, from bare provision to complex liturgies. The reasons for it have varied, including such factors as persecution, calendrical theories, and the shortage of priests. It has occurred in a surprising number of churches, Eastern Orthodox, Oriental, Roman Catholic, Old Catholic[1], Anglican, Catholic Apostolic and Presbyterian. Perhaps what they all have in common is a strong sense of consecration to undergird the practice.

This is not a book about communion for the sick (a closely related issue), nor about reservation (to which it is necessarily linked), nor about the eucharistic cultus. Other books have been written on these subjects and constraints of space exclude their discussion. The focus is on communion outside the eucharist both in the Anglican Communion and in the other churches. As yet there are many unresolved issues, and thus conclusions can only be provisional. But it does look as if there will continue to be authorization of such rites. This study aims to further the contemporary discussion.

One Sunday, while a lay chaplain in Northern Uganda, I discovered that the only priest available had to take the bus to Kampala leaving one hour before our weekly college eucharist. The priest consecrated the elements before leaving and I led the service of 'Communion under Special Circumstances' from the BCP 1979 (ECUSA). This was before I had ever heard of 'extended communion'. While a deacon I took consecrated elements to groups of old people. They were not sick, but lived in institutional homes, a grey area in official Church of England provision. On moving to Banbury, I began to work with women deacons who had been involved in 'extended communion' for a decade or more, and we are surrounded by villages, some of which have permission for communion by extension. I also find myself sharing a building with a Roman Catholic congregation who have a large number of 'eucharistic ministers' and therefore are able to keep up a daily communion by 'eucharistic services' when the priest is on holiday. Thus communion outside the eucharist has been a regular experience for a number of years.

This study begins with the early church, looking at the practice of 'home communion' and its development into liturgies of the presanctified, the western form of which has been undergoing revival in some provinces of the Anglican Communion. The Roman Catholic practice is examined; important as a comparison with Anglicanism. Then chapters on the Anglican Communion examine the practice in a number of provinces, but are by no means exhaustive. Theological issues arising from the liturgies are aired. As the texts for the services are found in a number of small pamphlets, the last chapter tries to bring together as many as space allows.

[1] Katholischen Bistrum der Alt-Katholiken in Deutschland, *Die Feier des Gottesdienst* (Bonn, 1981), pp.33-35.

Extended Communion in the Early Church 5

2. Extended Communion in the Early Church

The practice of home communion in the early church is well documented, and it is linked with communion for the sick and dying, and with the use of the sacrament for healing and protection.[1] We will concentrate on those writings that talk of home communion, but the evidence needs to be put alongside that of the sick, to see that private reservation seems to have been a common practice. Two forms of extended communion can be identified, domestic and monastic.

DOMESTIC COMMUNION

Twice in his *First Apology* Justin Martyr mentions that the deacons take the consecrated elements out from the service.

> 'those whom we call deacons give to each one present a portion of the bread and wine and water over which thanks have been given, and take them to those who are not present.
>
> everyone participates in (the elements) over which thanks have been given; and they are sent through the deacons to those who are not present.'[2]

The reasons for absence are not given, but presumably it could include sickness or imprisonment, or be due to work or slavery. This is not yet fully developed home communion, as Freestone comments:

> 'The purpose of the practice was to secure the participation of all the faithful in the one Eucharist: it was in no sense a private communion, but rather a local extension of the public service, as nearly coincident with the open communion as might be.'[3]

He therefore concludes that private reservation 'came into general use after the time of Justin.'[4]

By the time of the *Apostolic Tradition* this further step has been taken, for it includes regulations on the protection of the eucharist.

> '37 Let everyone take care that no unbeliever eats of the eucharist, nor any mouse or other animal, and that none of it falls and is lost. For it is the body of Christ . . .
>
> 38 For having blessed (the cup) in the name of God, you received as it were the antitype of the blood of Christ. Therefore do not pour it out, as though you despised it, lest an alien spirit lick it up.'[5]

---

[1] W. H. Freestone, *The Sacrament Reserved* (Mowbray, London, 1917).
[2] R. C. D. Jasper and G. J. Cuming, *Prayers of the Eucharist* (OUP, New York, 1980), pp.19-29.
[3] W. H. Freestone, *op. cit.*, p.33.
[4] *ibid.*, p.33.
[5] G. J. Cuming, *Hippolytus A Text for Students* (Grove Books, Bramcote, 1976), pp.27-28.

This seems to refer to reservation for communion 'in the home, apart from the liturgical assembly'[1], with the communicant blessing the cup. It is not clear how this was done. Cuming makes reference to the liturgy of the presanctified, and Mitchell interprets this to mean dropping a small piece of the consecrated bread into the cup.[2] Later the *Canons of Hippolytus* reinterpret this passage 'to be referring not to the communion from the reserved sacrament at home, but to the reception of the sacrament in church'[3], a clericalization of this passage.

Tertullian twice refers to home communion. In his letter *To his wife* he tells her not to marry a pagan in the event of his death.

'Will your husband know what it is that you taste in secret before (eating) any food? And will anyone, not knowing the reason of these things, endure them without murmuring? without wondering whether it be bread or a charm?'[4]

In *On Prayer* he also discusses the nature of fast days and suggests that those who have scruples about receiving the eucharist on such days do not absent themselves from the assembly, but rather carry the consecrated elements home to partake of them after the fast.[5] Taft comments:

'it was customary for the faithful to take from it [the Sunday synaxis] enough of the blessed gifts for communion during the week. The evidence for this from Tertullian is unquestionable.'[6]

Cyprian possibly refers to lay reservation in *The Lapsed*, and in a letter exhorts:

'A severer and fiercer combat is now threatening for which . . . the soldiers of Christ ought to prepare themselves, considering, therefore, that they daily drink the chalice of the blood of Christ so that they themselves may also be able to shed their blood for Christ.'[7]

Mitchell comments on this,

'It is possible that Cyprian is here referring not to a daily eucharistic liturgy, but to the custom of receiving communion daily at home.'[8]

Certainly Cyprian knew of home reservation, and protective uses of the sacrament.[9] But Callum sees here a daily Mass, although he admits that texts are ambiguous, and says 'nothing prevents the simultaneous existence of daily Mass and private Communion.'[10]

[1] N. Mitchell, *Cult and Controversy: The Worship of the Eucharist outside the Mass* (Pueblo, New York, 1982), p.219.
[2] G. J. Cuming, *op. cit.* p.27; see N. Mitchell, *op. cit.*, p.12.
[3] P. F. Bradshaw (ed.), *The Canons of Hippolytus* (Grove Books, Bramcote, 1987), p.30.
[4] W. H. Freestone, *op. cit.*, p.37.
[5] N. Mitchell, *op. cit.*, p.14.
[6] R. Taft, *Beyond East and West* (Pastoral Press, Washington, 1984), p.62.
[7] N. Mitchell, *op. cit.*, p.13.
[8] *ibid.*, p.13.
[9] *ibid.*, pp.12-13.
[10] D. Callum, 'The frequency of Mass in the Latin Church ca. 400' in *Theological Studies*, 45 (1984), p.616.

Basil writes about home communion and of the practice of the monks.

'It is not necessary to point out that for anyone to be obliged in times of persecution to take the communion with his own hand, when no priest or deacon is present, is not a serious offence; for a longstanding custom has found a sanction for the practice in the actual circumstances. All the solitaries in the deserts, where there is no priest, keep the communion by them and partake of it by themselves. At Alexandria too, and in Egypt, each one of the laity, for the most part, keeps the communion at home, and whenever he wishes partakes of it by himself. For, after the priest has competed the sacrifice once and distributed it, he who then receives it . . . when he partakes of it each time, must believe that he duly take and receives it from the hand that first gave it.'[1]

Basil thus looks back to the practice of home communion as a longstanding custom. He links it to persecution, although his concern seems to be to assuage fears about laity touching the elements, suggesting increased clericalization by his time. He also begins to articulate a theology about the connection between the home communion and the liturgy, an issue that is never far from communion outside the eucharist.

Early monasticism was a lay movement and as such communities may not have included a priest. The sixth century *Rule of the Master* envisages a situation in which:

'Communion *extra missam* seems to have been performed . . . As for the eucharistic sacrifice, the monks appear to have attended it only on Sundays, and doubtless went to the parish church to do so. Mass was celebrated in the oratory of the monastery only on rare and special occasions, when the secular clergy were invited.'[2]

The description in the Rule of the rite of communion will be discussed later in this chapter.

Increasing numbers of priest-monks led to a decline in extended communion, nevertheless it prevailed for a surprisingly long time in a variety of forms.[3] In particular, the situation in women's religious communities could require a communion service. Some Jacobite bishops from Persia exiled in Antioch (532-534) explained the practice of their communities:

'The custom of the East, namely, that the superiors of female monasteries should be deaconesses and should share the mysteries with those who are under their power, should be preserved everywhere there is a deaconess, if there is no priest or deacon in the place where the mysteries are shared.'[4]

Martimort sees this as parallel to the position of *Testamentum Domini*, where the deaconess takes the communion to sick.[5]

[1] W. H. Freestone, *op. cit.*, p.41.
[2] A. de Vogüé, 'Problems of the Monastic Conventual Mass', *Downside Review*, 87 (1969), p.328.
[3] W. H. Freestone, *op. cit.*, cb. 5 p.51ff.
[4] G. Martimort, *Deaconesses* (Ignatius Press, San Francisco, 1986, 1986), p.140.
[5] *ibid.*, p.140.

PROHIBITION OF COMMUNION OUTSIDE THE CHURCH

Bradshaw says that 'regulations provide excellent evidence for what was actually happening in local congregations, not by what is decreed should be done but by what is either directly prohibited or indirectly implied should cease to be done'.[1] Home communion is not without its prohibitions and those who write against it.

Jerome complained that those who were excluded in church were receiving communion at home. 'What is not allowed in church is not allowed at home . . . Let each one examine himself and then approach the body of Christ.'[2] This is not against home communion as such but indicates one of the reasons for increasing legislation against it.

The Council of Saragossa (c.379-381) passed the resolution, 'if anyone is found guilty of not consuming in church the eucharist he has received, let him be anathema.'[3] A council of bishops in Toledo (c.400) promulgated, 'if anyone does not consume the eucharist that he receives from the priest, he is to be expelled as sacrilegious.'[4] Thus Spain seems to have turned against the practice of home communion. The Council in Rouen (650) instructs, the clergy to place the eucharist not in the hands but only into the mouth. Mitchell sees this 'to be an implicit prohibition against eucharistic reservation by laity in their homes.'[5] But Callum sees 'no compelling reason for connecting these canons with the private reception of Communion.'[6]

Canon 58 of the Council in Trullo (692) forbids the laity to distribute the communion whenever clergy are present, and canon 101 forbids the putting of the elements into special vessels at the communion, both of which Freestone sees as nails in the coffin of domestic communion.[7] Nevertheless John Moschus writes of home communion by laity in the seventh century.[8] Symeon of Thessalonica talks of self-communion by monks in the fifteenth century, and the practice continued for another two centuries in the Russian church.[9]

ORIGINS OF COMMUNION AT HOME

Freestone concludes that:

'The practice seems to have been fairly general. Writers from the third century on allude to it as a familiar custom. The references are not numerous, it is true, but they include Rome, Africa, Alexandria, Syria and Macedonia. We know from the fact that action was taken to suppress private reservation among the laity by two Spanish councils at the end of the fourth century, that it had reached that part of the world before that date.'[10]

---

[1] P. Bradshaw, *The Search for the Origins of Christian Worship* (SPCK, London, 1992) p.69.
[2] N. Mitchell,*op. cit.*, p.17.
[3] *ibid.*, p.18-19.
[4] W. H. Freestone, *op. cit.*, p.48.
[5] N. Mitchell, *op. cit.*, p.278.
[6] D. Callum, *op. cit.*, p.626.
[7] W. H. Freestone, *op. cit.*, pp.226-227.
[8] *ibid.*, p.278.
[9] N. Uspensky, *Evening Worship* (SVS Press, Crestwood, 1985), p.119.
[10] W. H. Freestone, *op. cit.*, p.45.

Callum is more cautious, but his study only covers the Latin church.[1] What factors caused the rise of the practice? The first, which Freestone champions[1] is that of persecution. 'The origin of private reservation among the laity is closely bound up with the period of persecution.'[2] Evidence for this can be seen in the letter of Basil and in the comments of Cyprian on Christian courage. But other factors may be involved.

Mitchell talks of the separation of the eucharist from the communal meal.[3] This had already begun in the New Testament with the division of the eucharist and the agape, which changes the stress from a communal meal to the holy food. The practice seen in Justin Martyr of taking the consecrated elements to those not present (probably for good pastoral reasons) strengthens this trend, dividing consumption from the assembly. Mitchell sees adoration and benediction as a logical development of this division. But is this logical, when contrasted with the Orthodox? Schmemann says, 'the preservation of the Gifts as reserved sacrament, used for Communion of the sick . . . is a self-evident tradition' but that the Orthodox tradition has 'no adoration of the Eucharistic gifts outside of Communion.'[4]

Uspensky points to the teaching of the fathers on the Lord's Prayer.[5] Tertullian, Cyprian and Cyril of Jerusalem all give a sacramental interpretation to 'give us this day our daily bread'. It would seem that the daily eucharist is a later development, and that (particularly in the case of Tertullian) this was fulfilled by domestic communion, the elements being taken from the Sunday eucharist.

If these factors combined to encourage home communion (both domestic and monastic), then others led to its decline. In part there may have been a greater clericalization with the end of persecution.[6] The filling of the liturgical calendar led to greater frequency of celebration of the eucharist. Awe at the holy food led to a decline in the reception of communion not only at home but even at the Sunday celebration. Yet, even in the face of these factors, communion outside the eucharist has continued to happen, as will be seen in later chapters.

LITURGY FOR HOME COMMUNION

There is very little evidence of any liturgy for home communion outside monasticism. Uspensky sees in the story of the last communion of Mary of Egypt (d.522) an 'elemental order of service'.

> 'When the elder Zosima brought her holy communion, Mary asked him to recite the Creed and the "Our Father". After this she kissed the old man and took communion. Then she raised her hands towards heaven . . . and said: "Lord, now lettest Thou Thy servant . . ."'[7]

---

[1] D. Callum, *op. cit.*, pp.613-614.
[2] W. H. Freestone, *op. cit.*, p.44.
[3] N. Mitchell, *op. cit.*, pp.16-29.
[4] A. Schmemann, *Great Lent*, (SVS Press, Crestwood, 1990), p.59.
[5] N. Uspensky, *op. cit.*, pp.121-122.
[6] See comments on *Canons of Hippolytus* above.
[7] N. Uspensky, *op. cit.*, p.119.

Uspensky regards the creed and the Lord's Prayer as constituting the fundamental order.

The Rule of the Master gives a description of the way communion is to happen in the monastery ...[1]

The Rule of the Master
In the Oratory
the sign of peace
the abbot's communion
servers' communion
dean and deanery's communion
In the Refectory
the abbot's prayers
lowering of basket
abbot signs the bread and breaks it
distribution of blessed bread
distribution of cups of unmixed wine
blessing of food
community meal

Communion and the community meal are connected. Communion takes place after none and before the meal. Both elements are received and administered by a layman (the abbot). The rule is very concerned for reception to happen in the correct hierarchical order. Communion is followed by an elaborate meal ritual beginning with the abbot blessing bread lowered to him in a basket. It is not clear to what extent this rule was followed by communities, and although this Rule is a source, this section is not included in the *Rule of St Benedict*. It would seem possible to say that, in the west, monastic communion outside the eucharist occurred and that the *Rule of the Master* gives some idea of what that might have been like.

In the *Horologion of St. Sabbas the Sanctified* we have the first rite of communion outside the eucharist.[2] This rite is the origin of the present office of *The Typica* still found in the Byzantine ritual. The *Horologion* implies that the distribution of communion took place after the ninth hour.

The Typica is appointed to be said after the ninth hour, but its role as a rite of communion outside the eucharist had been taken over by the Liturgy of the Presanctified.[3] As can be seen in the table overleaf on page 12, the communion prayers of *The Horologion* have been omitted in *The Typica* and office material added, but the close connection of the two rites can be seen.

---

[1] *Rule of the Master* (Cistercian Publications, Kalamazoo, 1977), pp.171-177.
[2] N. Uspensky, *op. cit.*, p.123.
[3] Mother Mary Arch. K. Ware, *The Lenten Triodion* (Faber, London, 1978), p.87.

Horologion of St. Sabbas the Sanctified	The Typica
Remember us ...	Remember us ...
Beatitudes	Beatitudes
Remember us ...	Remember us ...
The choir of heaven hymns	Troparia: The heavenly choir sings
Nicene Creed	Nicene Creed
	Prayer for forgiveness
Lord's Prayer	Lord's Prayer
	Kontakion (variable)
Kyrie	Kyrie
One is holy	
Taste and see	
(communion anthems)	
Prayer after communion	
Prayer of thanksgiving	
	Glory be ...
	Greater in honour
	In the name
	God be merciful
	Prayer of St. Ephrem
	(Prayers
	Dismissal)

OBSERVATIONS

Persecution seems to have been the context for the development of home communion. It ceased domestically, but continued in monasteries. As some priests became monks so monastic communion also fell into desuetude. Today at Taizé communion is given after the morning office. In some ways, not least in its simplicity, this reflects monastic communion of the early church. However the reasons for the practice in Taizé are different; those of a modern ecumenical community.

3. Liturgies of the Presanctified

The origins of this liturgy are linked to questions about fasting, an issue seen in Tertullian. Canon 52 in Trullo prohibits the eucharist in Lent but says that the Liturgy of the Presanctified should be celebrated.[1] Bar Hebraeus names Severos of Antioch as the founder of the rite:

'since the canons prescribe that the oblation be discontinued in the Great Fast, the faithful asked the blessed Mar Severus that they might communicate: and he ... arranged that they should leave over the oblation that had been perfected on the Sunday, and therefrom communicate.'[2]

Although the Byzantine rite ascribes authorship to Gregory the Theologian, Uspensky supports Severos.[3] Thus its origin is in the theology of Lent (and therefore fasting) rather than due to factors such as persecution. Nevertheless, Uspensky sees this liturgy as a direct development of the practice of home communion, 'the replacement of private communion by a rite of public communion in church.'[4] Today it is found as a living reality in the Byzantine tradition, in the Maronite church, and in Western provision for Good Friday.[5]

---

[1] R. Taft, op. cit., p.67.
[2] H. W. Codrington, 'The Syrian Liturgies of the Presanctified II' in *Journal of Theological Studies*' Vol. V (1904), p.371.
[3] J. Ryan and J. de Uinck, *Byzantine Daily Worship* (Alleluia Press, Allendale, 1969), p.349; N. Uspensky op. cit., pp.143-144.
[4] ibid., p.139, cf. p.143.
[5] W. J. Grisbrooke, 'Presanctified Mass', J. G. Davies (ed.), in *A New Dictionary of Liturgy and Worship*, (SCM, London, 1986), pp.444-446.

BYZANTINE

The Liturgy of the Presanctified is celebrated on Wednesdays and Fridays in Lent. It occurs in the evening as the service breaking the lenten fast. The Liturgy is a combination of the office of vespers with a rite of communion.

Byzantine
Liturgy of the Presanctified
Vespers
Blessing
Ps 103
Lamp lighting prayer
Vesper Psalms
Preparation of the holy gifts
Great incensing
Little entrance
O Joyful Light!
Lessons with Ps 141
Gospel
Communion
Litanies (including for those ready for illumination)
Entrance of the Holy Gifts
Lord's Prayer
Elevation
Fraction
Placing of particles in chalice
Communion
Concluding rites

The bread is consecrated on Sunday and prepared in silence during the vesper psalms. The litanies and lessons have their origins in preparing catechumens, not least the litany and dismissal of those who are ready for illumination (baptism). Then comes the Entrance of the Holy Gifts with the prostration of the people. The rite continues with the actions of the eucharist, elevation, 'holy presanctified things for the holy', and fraction. Wine is not reserved from Sunday, but rather a particle of the preconsecrated bread is dropped into the chalice, which is seen as consecratory. Patriarch Michael comments on this action saying,

'the holy bread which has been presanctified and made perfect earlier is placed into the mystical chalice, and the wine contained in it is transformed into the holy blood of our Lord.'[1]

---

[1] *ibid.*, pp.148-149.

Later versions of the Good Friday liturgy in the west reserved in only one kind and consecrated by intinction.[1] The clergy and people then receive communion and the Presanctified Liturgy is completed with the post-communion rites. The service is led by a priest and a deacon.

MARONITE AND SYRIAN
The only Liturgy of the Presanctified remaining in the Syrian tradition is on Maronite Good Friday. There is much manuscript evidence for presanctified liturgies in the Syrian Orthodox and East Syrian traditions but these have fallen into desuetude.[2] The following is the outline of the Maronite rite, which happens after the ninth hour.

Maronite
Great Friday: Signing the Chalice
Preparation of the Chalice
Doxology
Opening prayer
Ps 51
Hoosoyo (Proemion and Sedro)
Trisagion
Mazmooro
Readings
Transfer of the Chalice
Diaconal proclamations
Hymn of transfer
Prayer for the dead
Creed
(Washing of the hands)
Signing the Chalice
Rite of peace
Blessing with the veil
Commemorations
Dialogue
Epiclesis
Signing of the chalice
Lord's prayer
Penitential rite
Communion rite
Thanksgiving
Dismissal

[1] R. F. Buxton, *Eucharist and Institution Narrative* (Mayhew McCrimmon, Great Wakering, 1976), pp.36-37.
[2] H. W. Codrington, 'The Syrian Liturgies of the Presanctified' in *Journal of Theological Studies*, Vol. IV (1903), pp.69-82; 'The Syrian Liturgies of the Presanctified III' in *Journal of Theological Studies*, Vol. V (1904), pp.535-545.

As in the Byzantine rite, only the bread is reserved. The signing is seen as consecrating the wine. This is made clear by the prayers of the service. The sedro asks:
'consecrate this chalice mixed with wine and water by the sanctifying union of your holy body.'[1]
The epiclesis says:
'May he [the Spirit] rest upon this chalice to bless and sanctify it by the mystery of the Holy Trinity.'[2]
At the signing the priest says:
'now we seal and sign + the chalice of salvation with the purifying ember which glows with heavenly Mysteries.'[3]
The Maronite rite is more elaborate and explicit at this point than the Byzantine simplicity.

It would seem that the latinization of the Maronite liturgy by the development of a daily eucharist led to the signing of the chalice being limited to Good Friday. Although the Chaldean Breviary includes a presanctified Mass in Lent, this has ceased. Vellian shows that later prohibitions on reservation also hindered the practice.[4] The Syrian Orthodox no longer celebrate the presanctified. Only on the Wednesday of Mid-Lent and the feast of the Annunciation is the Qurbana offered during the Great Fast.

WESTERN: GOOD FRIDAY
Callum believes western daily Mass to have its origin in home communion.[5] It inhibited the development of the Liturgy of the Presanctified, except on Good Friday in which elements consecrated on Maundy Thursday are distributed. Dix also saw this latter practice as 'a survival, unchanged in popular devotion . . . of communion *at home*'.[6]

The table opposite of Good Friday rituals compares the Roman Rite (1975), the ecumenical Joint Liturgical Group Services (1983), and Anglican rites from the United States (BCP 1979), Canada (BAS 1985), England (*Lent—Holy Week—Easter* 1986) and Southern Africa (APB 1989). These all have a common structure, a simple ministry of the word with intercessions, the 'veneration' of the cross, and a rite of communion. Anglican rites have most difficulty with the second section, which they label differently as devotions, meditation, proclamation or adoration.

The rite of communion is very simple. The Roman rite has a transfer of the gifts from the chapel of repose. Anglican rites try to make this as simple as possible. Then there are varying rites of communion based on the eucharistic liturgy. The JLG rite reduced everything to an optional rubric; it would seem that communion extended from the Maundy Thursday liturgy is not common in English Free Churches.

---

[1] Diocese of St. Maron, *The Maronite Liturgical Year* Vol. III (Diocese of St. Maron, 1982), p.153
[2] *ibid.*, p.164.
[3] *ibid.*, p.166.
[4] J. Vellian, *East Syrian Evening Services* (K. P. Press, Kottayam, 1971) pp.28-29.
[5] D. Callum, *op. cit.*, p.650.
[6] G. Dix, *The Shape of the Liturgy* (Dacre Press, Westminster, 1945), p.441.

Western: Good Friday					
Rome 1975	ECUSA 1979	JLG 1983	BAS 1985	L·HW·E 1986	APB 1989
Word					
	(Greeting)		Versicle		
Collect	Collect	Collect	Collects	Collect	Collect
Isaiah	OT	Isaiah	Isaiah	Isaiah	Isaiah
Ps 30	Ps	Ps 88	Ps 22	Ps 22	Ps 31
Hebrews	Hebrews	Hebrews	Hebrews	Hebrews	Hebrews
Acclamation		Ps 54		Hymn	Acclamation
John 18	John 18	John 18	John 18	John 18	John 18
	Sermon	Sermon	(Sermon)	Sermon	(Sermon)
General Intercessions	Solemn Collects	Intercessions	Solemn Intercessions		General Intercessions
Cross					
Invitation					
Veneration	Devotions		Meditation	Proclamation	Adoration
Songs	Anthems	(Anthems)	Anthems	Anthems	Anthems
				Intercessions	
Communion					
Transfer			Placing	Placing	
	Confession				
Lord's Prayer	Lord's Prayer		Lord's Prayer	Lord's Prayer	Lord's Prayer
Priest's Prayer					
				Jesus Lamb of God	Jesus Lamb of God
					Humble Access
				Invitation	Invitation
This is the Lamb			Gifts of God	Jesus is the Lamb	
Communion	Communion	(Communion)	Communion	Communion	Communion
Collect	Collect	(Collect)	Collects	Collect	Collect
Prayer over people			Prayer over people		Prayer over people

In common with the liturgies of the presanctified in the eastern rites, the impetus for this liturgy is to do with the calendar, this time not Lent, but Good Friday. As Gordon Wakefield says about this day, 'the crucial and controversial question is "Eucharist or no?" '[1] The Church of England made provision for both, as *Lent—Holy Week—Easter* included, as an option the Good Friday Liturgy of the Presanctified.[2] This seems to be acceptable even in the evangelical wing of the church. 'Communion from the sacrament consecrated on Maundy Thursday is ... provided for on the continuum argument, that this partaking is simply an extension of the Maundy Thursday service.'[3]

OBSERVATIONS
Observations In the Liturgies of the Presanctified the issue has been one of calendar: is it appropriate to celebrate the eucharist on a particular day? How can we not hold a eucharist and yet receive our 'daily bread'? Tertullian answered the question with reference to the practice of home communion of his day. Severus of Antioch seems to have replied by creating the Liturgy of the Presanctified, a parish rather than domestic rite, which continues in the Byzantine tradition. This rite has influenced 'The Community of the Servants of the Will of God' an Anglican monastic order who celebrate a modified version of the Byzantine ritual on Wednesdays in Lent and on Fridays outside of Christmas and Eastertide.[4] Although the Maronites have the daily eucharist in Lent, they resort to the Syrian Signing the Chalice on Good Friday.

The Liturgy of the Presanctified is a combination of office and communion. This contrasts with the western rites of extended communion to be examined next, which modify the eucharistic liturgy. The Presanctified also includes entrance, elevation and fraction, elements often omitted from modern western services. This suggests a strong conception of continuity between the Presanctified and the Liturgy. Modern communion rites seem to suffer angst about discontinuity.

In the west, Rome continued the tradition of the Presanctified for Good Friday. Recently this has seen an official revival in many parts of Anglicanism. Thus many churches hold that on certain days it is not right to celebrate the eucharist, but each tradition has different opinions of which days are aliturgical and the nature of the rite for such a day.

---

[1] G. S. Wakefield, 'Holy Week' in *Holy Week Services* (SPCK, London, 1971, 1983), p.16.
[2] *Lent—Holy Week—Easter* (SPCK, London, 1984, 1986) p.197.
[3] T. Lloyd, *Celebrating Lent, Holy Week, Easter* (Grove Worship Series no. 93, Grove Books, Bramcote, 1985), p.22.
[4] Monastery of the Holy Trinity, *The Liturgy of the Presanctified* (Crawley Down 1986).

4. The Roman Catholic Church

There have been various uses of the sacrament in rites of communion in the Roman tradition including the *fermentum*[1] and 'communion after mass.'[2] It was not until after Trent that official rites were developed for Communion outside the Mass. The rubrics and introductions to these rites shows the changing pastoral context, not least the growing impact of the shortage of priests. 'Eucharistic Services' are now common in many parts of the world. The Vatican *Directory* seems to be preparing for the Mass as such to cease to be the normal Sunday service, being replaced by rites of communion.[3] Indeed this is already happening.

THE RITE OF DISTRIBUTING HOLY COMMUNION OUTSIDE MASS 1614, 1974
The 1614 ritual was very bare, which can be seen in the table contrasting it with the two 1974 rites; all however follow a common outline.

1614 Ritual	1974 ICEL Ritual	
	Long Form	Short Form
	Introductory Rites	
	Greeting —for priest/deacon —for laity	Greeting —for priest/deacon —for laity
Confession/Absolution	Penitential Rite	Penitential Rite
	Liturgy of the Word	
	Celebration of the Word of God (Mass readings and intercessions)	Short form of reading the Word (Short scriptural text)
	Communion Rites	
	Our Father	Our Father
	The peace	
Behold the Lamb ...	This is the Lamb ...	This is the Lamb ...
Communion	Communion	Communion
	Silence or song	Silence or song
Concluding prayer	Concluding prayer	Concluding prayer
	Concluding Rites	
Blessing	Blessing —by a priest/deacon —by laity	Blessing —by a priest/deacon —by laity
	Dismissal	Dismissal

[1] W. H. Freestone, *op. cit.*, pp.73-77 and G. P. Jeanes (ed.), *The Origins of the Roman Rite* (Alcuin/GROW Joint Liturgical Study no. 20, Grove Books, Bramcote, 1991), p.45.
[2] N. Mitchell, *op. cit.*, pp.226-231.
[3] The *Directory* has led to the services being designated 'SWOP' (Sunday WithOut a Priest!).

The introduction to the 1974 services says the faithful 'even when they receive communion outside Mass . . . are closely united with the sacrifice . . . of the cross . . . [and] are sharers in the sacred banquet.'[1] So the faithful may petition the priest for communion, if they are unable to go to Mass. But they are told 'sacramental communion received during Mass is the most perfect participation in the eucharistic celebration.'[2]

The General Introduction states that 'the primary and original reason for reservation of the eucharist outside the Mass is the administration of viaticum.'[3] But Communion outside the Mass is connected in The Rites to other practices, including the eucharistic cultus.

The 1614 and 1974 rites presuppose a context in which priests are freely available. The 1974 service, based on the Mass, provides for those laity who have not been able to attend Mass. Options are given for it to be led by a priest or deacon, or layperson. If the service is led by a priest or deacon, it concludes with a blessing 'May almighty God bless you . . .'. Laypersons have to use blessings in 'us' form. There is a clear omission of anything like a eucharistic prayer, the service moving directly from the intercessions to the Lord's Prayer.

Roman Catholic parishes have increasingly taken advantage of this provision, even in circumstances where there is no shortage of priests. In England lay people are trained in their parish and commissioned by the priest for this ministry.[4] Thus in the absence of the priest (perhaps for a holiday or day off) lay people lead eucharistic services and thereby maintain the tradition of daily communion. But this service has also been adapted in parts of the world where the shortage of priests is severe.

EUCHARISTIC SERVICES
The following table compares three Catholic rites used in different episcopal conferences, and the comments of the Vatican *Directory*.

Gotteslob 1975	Sunday Celebrations 1976	Ritual For Lay Presiders 1984	Directory in the Absence of a Priest 1988
Introductory Rites			
Song		Song	
Greeting	Greeting	Greeting	Greeting
Introduction	Penitential rite (5 forms)	Penitential rite (5 forms)	Penitential rite
	Hymn (or Gloria)	Gloria	
Prayer	Prayer	Opening prayer (7 additional forms)	

[1] *The Rites* (Pueblo, New York, 1976, 1983), p.479-480.
[2] *ibid.*, p.479.
[3] *ibid.*, p.476.
[4] F. Lobinger, *Training Assistant Ministers of the Eucharist* (Collins, London, 1977, 1978).

continued from page 20

[1975]	[1976]	[1984]	[1988]
Liturgy of the Word			
Reading	Reading	First Reading	First Reading
Responsorial Psalm	Psalm	Responsorial Psalm	Psalm
		Second Reading	Second Reading
		Gospel acclamation	Gospel acclamation
Gospel	Gospel	Gospel	Gospel
Homily	Period of meditation	Shared reflection	Homily
Profession of faith	Profession of faith (Nicene or Apostles Creed)	Profession of faith (3 forms)	Profession of faith
Prayer of the community Praise—thanksgiving —confession— biddings—doxology	General intercessions (3 forms)	General intercessions (7 forms) and collection	General intercessions (including for vocations, bishop and parish priest)
The Thanksgiving			
	Prayer of Praise and Thanksgiving (4 forms)	Thanksgiving (8 forms)	Thanksgiving Psalm Canticle or Litany or eucharistic hymn
Communion Rites			
Prayer of unity with the Church Prayer of unity with one another			
Collection			
Our Father	Our Father	Our Father	Our Father
		Peace	Peace
This is the Lamb	Word of invitation (2 forms)	Admonition to unity (2 forms)	This is the Lamb ...
Communion	Communion	Communion	Communion
Prayer or song of thanks	Silent prayer or song	Silence or song	Silence or song
	Concluding prayer	Prayer after communion (7 additional forms)	Concluding prayer
Concluding Rites			
Notices—Blessing Song (to Mary)	Blessing and dismissal	Blessing (11 forms) and dismissal	Blessing and dismissal

GOTTESLOB 1975

After the Communist occupation in 1945, the Catholic church in East Germany had to rely, in some places, on not very popular Bible services. In 1965 they were given permission to add to this the distribution of communion. *Eucharisticum Mysterium* (1967) allowed lay folk to distribute communion and so regularized the German practice. The shortage of priests in West Germany encouraged the German bishops to extend the practice to the west and a rite for distributing communion was incorporated into the hymn and service book *Gotteslob* (1975). This book is currently used in Germany and Austria.[1]

Graf comments, 'communion outside the Mass is certainly not a fore-runner of the new communion services of entire communities on Sundays'.[2] The distinction he makes is that the previous services were quasi-private affairs alongside the Mass, as the main Sunday celebration. He denies that the Liturgy of the Presanctified is a fore-runner, for this is a mid-week service. Ecumenically the services are seen as disastrous, dissolving the unity of the word and the sacrament.

Elements of thanksgiving are included in the 'prayer of the community'. The praise is the Gloria. There is a short thanksgiving prayer, followed by a penitential sentence then various biddings. These prayers conclude with the doxology of the Gloria. The prayer of unity locates the assembly in the parish and diocese and under the Pope. Thus this is similar to the admonitions to unity we will see in other rites.

SUNDAY CELEBRATIONS 1976-1978

Sunday Celebrations is the ICEL translation of *Assemblées dominicales en l'absence du prêtre* from Le Centre National de Pastorale Liturgique, Paris. Denis Hurley in the preface to the English translation asserts that 'Sunday is the sole element of the Christian calendar which goes back without interruption to Jesus himself.'[3] He also says that 'Sunday has from the very beginning been characterized by the Lord's Supper or eucharist'.[4] His justification for eucharistic services is pragmatic 'when the parish priest is unable to be present . . . it is of the greatest importance that the local community gather to hear the Word and to partake of the Lord under eucharistic forms derived from a previous celebration.'[5]

In the preface of the French document, Marcel Descargues is more blunt about the situation. 'In many places, especially in rural communities, the Church is disappearing.'[6] He laments that many profess Christianity in a privatized way which 'in no way involves others'. He asserts Christians need to gather together to build up the living church and to 'make it visible to themselves and to others'.

---

[1] H. J. Graf, 'Priestless Sunday Services with Communion and Resulting Problems' in *East Asian Pastoral Review*, Vol. XVIII No. 2 (1981) pp.175-189.
[2] *ibid.*, pp.184-185.
[3] ICEL, *Sunday Celebrations* (Washington, 1978) p.5.
[4] *ibid.*, p.5.
[5] *ibid.*, p.6.
[6] *ibid.*, p.8.

This introduction shows us some of the difficulties of the church in France in the twentieth century. The vision of the preface is of a church which can only exist through the gathering together of Christian people. The next page reinforces this message with a quote from The Teachings of the Apostles: 'Bishop, exhort the people and persuade them to be faithful to the assembly; may they not fail in this. Let them gather and may no one diminish the church by not joining the assembly and thus deprive the body of Christ of one member.'[1]

Laity are to meet in the absence of a priest, and are exhorted to form a committee to plan their assemblies using the liturgy provided. The remarks ominously envisage the priest 'being unavailable for an extended period of time'.[2]

This service follows that of Holy Communion outside Mass, with additions and without the priestly options. 'Since the laity cannot take the place of the ordained priest' various parts have to be omitted, including the eucharistic prayer and the greeting 'The Lord be with you'. The blessing is in 'us' form. The Apostles Creed is an alternative to the Nicene creed and there are three suggestions for intercessions. Before communion two forms are given for 'words of invitation expressing the connection between this communion and the celebration of the Mass.'[3] But the most striking addition to Holy Communion outside Mass is the provision of four 'Prayers of Praise and Thanksgiving'.[4]

The directions are very permissive for these prayers. It is permitted to adapt the prayers according to circumstance. A well-known hymn or a poetic text may be used. To be avoided is anything 'which closely resembles a eucharistic prayer'. The thanksgivings avoid any reference to the Last Supper or the consecrated elements. The first gives thanks for the mighty acts of God in salvation history, others ponder the work of God in creation and community. Such prayers raise acute questions, not least: when is a thanksgiving a eucharistic prayer?

RITUAL FOR LAY PRESIDERS 1984

This document was produced by the Western Liturgical Conference of Canada.[5] The topic must not be confused with lay presidency; a lay presider is a layperson who leads a distribution rite. In the Prairies there are many small scattered communities and an acute shortage of priests. This book fills the gap and is more comprehensive than the French rite with a great variety of material. The eight thanksgivings provided are both seasonal and general. There is less reticence than in France to include thanksgiving for the eucharist. Indeed the main thanksgiving contains the paragraph 'appropriate when communion will be ministered':
'We thank you for the gift of the Eucharist, for the coming of your Son Jesus among us: one Lord, one holy bread of life, one holy and ever glorious body. By our communion in Christ, we are united with the whole Church. You make the salvation Jesus gained for us present here and now, as it was in the Upper Room, at the Last Supper, and as it was at Calvary . . .'[6]

---

[1] *ibid.*, p.9.
[2] *ibid.*, p.10.
[3] see Text 2 p.48 below.
[4] see Text 1 p.47 below.
[5] Western Liturgical Conference, *Ritual for Lay Presiders*, (St. Peter's Press, Saskatchewan, 1984).
[6] *ibid.*, p.10, and see Text 3 p.48 below.

The Roman Catholic Church 23

The service also includes an optional 'Admonition to Unity' to be declared from time to time. Both forms talk of being 'in special union with N our pastor.'[1] It is not exactly clear as to who this is, though it is presumably the parish priest, but there is no indication as to when the Mass was celebrated from which the elements have come. What is the nature of this special relationship to the pastor? It could be said that for most of the time the relationship is one of a 'real absence'. This contrasts with the introduction which asserts that:

'Leaders will come forward from the ranks of those adults who have been faithful to their baptism, confirmation and Eucharist. God's Holy Spirit will call them to new ministries, to new leadership.'[2]

But does not the leading of the Spirit include the calling to the office of priest?

DIRECTORY ON SUNDAY CELEBRATIONS IN THE ABSENCE OF A PRIEST 1988

This Vatican *Directory* seems to pave the way for priestless Sundays becoming a norm. The *Directory* talks of the peculiar contexts of first evangelization, and of persecution, but rather easily moves to parishes without the eucharist 'due to the drop in clergy numbers'.[3] It maintains that the eucharist performed by the priest is one of the principal elements of a Sunday celebration and sees the ideal solution being that the faithful travel to the Mass. When this is not practical, they should gather for the Word and for Eucharistic Communion. They should also pray:

'Give the church more priests
and keep them faithful in their love and service.'[4]

The Bishop is to oversee such assemblies, try to provide priests, make sure that the parish priest visits for penance and occasional celebrations of Mass.

The *Directory* is concerned that whoever presides should do so according to their station in the church. Deacons wear their vestments and bless. Lay persons must not take the place of the priest (an empty chair must remain), nor must they use the presidential greeting (the Lord be with you), bless in 'you' form, or use any part of the preparation and the eucharistic prayer. Any thanksgivings 'should not in any way take the form of a eucharistic prayer to avoid the danger of confusion'.[5] The host used can be consecrated on the same Sunday and brought by the minister, or can be that consecrated at the last mass in the church. Each Bishop's Conference is to give detailed plans for these celebrations. Thus we see the Vatican preparing the church for a situation that has already become the norm in some places, including France and Canada.

---

[1] *ibid.*, p.15, and see Text 4 p.49 below.
[2] *ibid.*, p.ii.
[3] Directory on Sunday Celebrations in the absence of a Priest, *Liturgy*, vol. 13 (Oct.-Nov. 1988), p.5.
[4] *ibid.*, p.9.
[5] *ibid.*, p.13.

OBSERVATIONS
The Roman Catholic Church has developed eucharistic services, at first in response to the inability of some of the laity to attend Mass, but latterly due to an increasing shortage of priests. In part this has been possible because of a clearly articulated theory of consecration, but also because of a traditional division in piety between eucharistic sacrifice and communion. Before Vatican II attendance at the sacrifice was most important. Now communion has been recovered, only to be sundered from the eucharist by the lack of priests.[1] R. W. Hovda regrets the development of this 'convenient habit' for it 'constitutes a continuing obstacle to appropriate disciplinary reforms'.[2] Does this include married priests?[3] Hovda is sad that the laity are content with second best, and do not press for the mass. The Roman Catholic situation needs to be considered carefully by Anglicans.

---

[1] F. J. van Beeck, 'Praise and Thanksgiving in Noneucharistic Communion Services' in *Worship*, vol. 60 (Sept. 1986), p.424.
[2] R. W. Hovda, 'The Amen Corner, "Priestless Sundays" Reconsidered' in *Worship*, vol. 62 (March, 1988), p.159.
[3] J. M. Huels, 'Chronicle: Sunday Liturgies Without Priest' in *Worship*, vol. 64 (Sept. 1990), p.460.

5. The Anglican Communion

The earliest example of extended communion in the Anglican Communion comes from eighteenth century Scotland. In other parts of Anglicanism it is unclear as to when the practice began, but the service books of the different Provinces show its occurrence. It became an item on the agenda of the Anglican Consultative Council, not least at ACC-7, which seemed to discourage the practice.[1] It was also discussed at the 1988 Lambeth Conference.[2] It is unknown in some places, e.g. Uganda, Kenya, and the Church of South India. In South Africa it is common, but no provision is made in the prayer book. In Brazil rubrics for deacons are given in their BCP[3], and Readers are automatically licensed to lead such communion services. In some Provinces individual dioceses have regulations.

THE SCOTTISH EPISCOPAL CHURCH 1764
The Scottish Episcopal Church contains the first example of extended communion in Anglicanism after the Reformation. From 1746 until 1792 Penal Laws were in place against the Church. It was illegal to possess a church or chapel and the maximum congregation allowed by law was five. In these circumstances communion from the reserved sacrament was common. Church life continued, and in 1764 the Scottish bishops issued an official version of the communion office.[4]

Between 1764 and 1776, bishop Alexander of Dunkeld used an alternative to the prayer of consecration when using the reserved sacrament (Text 5). This is based on the Scottish prayer but excludes any oblation of the consecrated elements.[5] An epiclesis is included upon those who are to communicate.

'... hear us, O merciful Father, we most humbly beseech thee, and of thy almighty goodness vouchsafe to bless with the Holy Spirit us (these) thy servants before thee, and to grant that we (they) receiving thy gifts and creatures of bread and wine already consecrated into the most precious body and blood of thy Son our Saviour J. + C. according to his holy institution, and in commemoration of his death and passion, may be partakers of all the benefits of the same ...'[6]

Thus were linked the last supper, consecration and reception, which in the 1764 rite are all at different times. Few have been able to hold all these together with the same economy. The prayer continues with phrases from the 1764 rite but also asks that the church 'may be delivered from the Devil and his snares'. Is this a reference to the London government?

---

[1] *Many Gifts One Spirit: Report of ACC-7 Singapore 1987*(CHP, London, 1987), p.57.
[2] The Lambeth Conference 1988, *The Truth Shall Make You Free* (ACC, London, 1989), p.73.
[3] Igreja Episcopal do Brasil, *Livro de Oração Comum* (1988), p.108.
[4] G. J. Cuming, *A History of Anglican Liturgy* (Macmillan, London, 1969), p.118.
[5] B. Wigan, *The Liturgy in English* (OUP, Oxford, 1962, 1964), pp.38-51.
[6] F. C. Eeles, *Traditional Ceremonial and Customs connected with the Scottish Liturgy* (Alcuin Club Collections XVII, Longmans Green & Co. 1910, pp.91-93.)

Although not Anglican, the English Catholic Apostolic leaders encouraged their members to become Anglicans as the church declined.[1] The church's liturgy contains an order of extended communion.[2] This seems to be a development of the Scottish Presbyterian tradition of Second Table communion, which is a service of administration of preconsecrated elements later in the day to those at a second sitting.[3] The Catholic Apostolic order includes a fine introduction (Text 6) and a prayer for 'the same inestimable benefits' which clearly connects the present action to that of the previous consecration, but does it in a prayer rather than in an exhortation or notice. This prayer shows the sacramental vision of the church:

'Thou hast accepted the offerings and sacrifice of Thy Church ... and through the ministry of Thine ordained servant, by the Holy Ghost, Thou hast made this bread and this cup to be the most precious Body and Blood of Christ our Saviour ... We beseech Thee, therefore, vouchsafe also unto these Thy servants the same inestimable benefits; that they, being admitted unto the same holy Communion, may receive remission of their sins ...'[1]

Thus is given one of the most clear explanations of extended communion of any rite produced. The following is the outline of the service.

Catholic Apostolic Church 1892
Order for the Administration of the Communion
Introduction (Text 6)
Confession
Absolution
Collect, Epistle, and Gospel
Nicene Creed
Prayer for 'the same inestimable benefits'
Christ our Passover ...
Humble Access
Agnus Dei
Prayer to Christ
Prayer to the Holy Ghost
Holy things ...
The Peace
(Benedictions)
Communion
Communion Anthem
Post-communion prayers
Gloria
Benediction

[1] K. W. Stevenson, 'The Catholic Apostolic Church—Its History and Its Eucharist' in *Studia Liturgica*, 13 (1978) pp.21-45.
[2] *The Liturgy, And other Divine Offices of the Church* (G. J. W. Pitman, London, 1892), pp.25-28.
[3] cf. *A New Directory for the Public Worship of God* (Macniven & Wallace, Edinburgh, 1898) pp.124-132.

ECUSA 1979

The Book of Common Prayer 1979 includes a service and a set of rubrics for the distribution from the reserved sacrament (Text 7). This was the first American prayer book to permit reservation although the practice already occurred in parishes. The service, *Communion under Special Circumstances,* is,

> 'intended not only for use with the sick . . ., but also with those who because of work schedules or other types of limitation cannot be present at public celebration.'[1]

The order is as follows.

BCP 1979
Communion under Special Circumstances
Scripture reading
Comment on reading
Prayers
Collect (of Maundy Thursday)
Confession
Absolution
Peace
Lord's prayer
Invitation (Sancta sanctis)
Administration
Post communion prayer
Blessing or dismissal

One analogy for extended communion used in the States has been that of a family birthday party, where if one member is sick, a piece of the birthday cake is sent to them. Indeed a similar thing happens in some places with wedding cake. 'A new cake wouldn't do at all. So, especially at Christmas and Easter, priests have for a long time reserved enough consecrated bread and wine'.[2]

The House of Bishops in 1965 gave permission for deacons to distribute Holy Communion in the absence of a priest. The rubrics therefore provide directions for such a service, which has led to the unfortunate title of 'deacons' mass'. These show how the service is to be modified, with the omission of all material preparing for the eucharist and the eucharistic prayer. After the Liturgy of the Word the service continues with the Lord's prayer and communion. Hatchett confidently asserts:

> 'deacons have administered to congregations from the reserved sacrament using the historic liturgy of the presanctified gifts.'[3]

---

[1] M. J. Hatchett, *Commentary on the American Prayer Book* (The Seabury Press, New York, 1981), p.408.
[2] C. P. Price, *Introducing the Proposed Book, Prayer Book Studies 29 Revised* (The Church Hymnal Corporation, New York, 1976), p.86.
[3] M. J. Hatchett, *op. cit.,* p.420.

This seems to overdo the evidence, as the eastern Liturgies of the Presanctified would normally be led by a priest. The provision is somewhat bare, but influential, due to this book being translated into Spanish and used in other Provinces. With the rise of the distinctive diaconate and local priests, these regulations are decreasingly used.

THE ANGLICAN CHURCH OF CANADA 1987

The Doctrine and Worship Committee were asked by the house of bishops to produce a service of *Public Distribution of Holy Communion by Deacons and Lay People*.[1] Each bishop authorizes the use of this rite in his or her diocese. The pastoral notes make clear that this is a 'temporary solution . . . which will make it possible for those who desire to be fed with both word and sacrament on a regular basis.'[2] Also 'the distribution of holy communion outside of the eucharist is not a substitute for a celebration of the eucharist . . . Holy Communion apart from the eucharist cannot replace the eucharist, but is an opportunity for the eucharist to reach into a context where the required conditions cannot, for the moment, be met.'[3] Three forms of service are provided and are shown in the table overleaf.

The leader of the service is called 'the presiding leader' or 'the presider', which seems to have the connotation of 'not quite the president'. Unlike Roman Catholic provision, no differentiation is made between the leader being a deacon or lay. The services follow as closely as possible their eucharistic parents, with the omission of the eucharistic prayer. There is no thanksgiving, nor is there any statement or prayer in the service which indicates when or where the elements were consecrated.

There are a number of good things about this service. Firstly, a clear procedure for the authorization of extended communion was developed. The bishops nationally approved a liturgy, and then each authorizes its use in his own diocese. This allows some dioceses to use a common rite, while others prohibit the practice. Secondly, by producing a booklet, the worshipper knows exactly what is happening. Confusion is inevitable in the mind of worshippers, if they are given a eucharistic service book, but the leader substitutes prayers for a service of extended communion. One weak point is in the omission of any suitable thanksgiving.

---

[1] Anglican Church of Canada, *Public Distribution of Holy Communion by Deacons and Lay People* (Anglican Book Centre, Toronto, 1987).
[2] *ibid.*, p.2.
[3] *ibid.*, p.3.

Public Distribution of Holy Communion by Deacons and Lay People		
Form 1 After BAS 1985	Form 2 After BCP 1962	Form 3 After BCP 1662
The Gathering of the Community		Lord's prayer
Greeting	Greeting	
Collect for Purity	Collect for Purity	Collect for Purity
	Summary of the law or 10 Commandments	10 Commandments or Summary of the law
Gloria		
Kyrie	Kyrie	Kyrie
Trisagion	Trisagion	
		Collect for the Queen
Collect of the Day	Collect of the Day	Collect of the Day
The Proclamation of the Word		
Readings	Readings	Epistle
Gospel	Gospel	Gospel
Sermon	Sermon	Nicene Creed
Nicene or Apostles Creed	Nicene Creed	Sermon
Prayers of the people	Prayers of the people	Intercession
Confession and prayer of forgiveness	Confession and prayer of forgiveness	Confession and prayer of forgiveness
		Comfortable words
The Peace	The Peace	The Peace
Holy Communion		
Lord's prayer	Lord's prayer	Lord's prayer
Gifts of God		
	Humble access	Humble access
Communion	Communion	Communion
		Agnus Dei
Prayer after communion	Prayer after communion	Prayer after communion
		Gloria
Dismissal	Dismissal	Dismissal

THE ANGLICAN CHURCH OF AUSTRALIA
A 1987 report for the Archbishop of Melbourne thoroughly looked into the issue.[1] 'Extended Communion appears to have spread unofficially in many dioceses . . . doubtless in response to the pressures of time and distance in country parishes'.[2] The report recorded some influential reflections by Gilbert Sinden, but concluded that the practice 'ought not to be encouraged'. Nevertheless it contained some liturgical suggestions.

The Archbishop of Brisbane sent out recommendations in 1988 and 1992, although the directions in his *Ad Clerum* 1992 suggest that he envisages the practice being rather rare. The two suggested orders set out in the table overleaf are based on *An Australian Prayer Book* 1978 and closely follow the Melbourne report.

The 1987 Melbourne report includes suggestions of what to do if the elements begin to run out, and emphatically bans the use of manual acts. It would appear that this provision is used in the country dioceses, but is less important in the cities. The diocese of Rockhampton, two and a half times the size of England, now has Ministry Teams whose role includes communion by extension.[3]

---

[1] *Extended Communion: A Report to the Archbishop of Melbourne* (1987). Information provided by Rev. Dr. C. Sherlock.
[2] *ibid.* p.1.
[3] *Guidelines for the Provision of Extended Communion*, Redrafted All Saints Day 1991 and *The Holy Communion by Extension*, Diocese of Rockhampton.

Brisbane 1988	
Suggested First Order	Suggested Second Order
Psalm/anthem/hymn	Psalm/canticle/hymn
Greeting	Greeting
Sentence	Sentence
Introduction	Introduction
Collect for Purity	Collect for Purity
10 Commandments or Summary of the Law or Kyrie	10 Commandments or Summary of the Law or Kyrie
	Gloria
Collect of the day	Collect of the day
Old Testament reading	Old Testament reading
Psalm/hymn/canticle	Psalm
Epistle	New Testament reading
	Hymn
Gospel	Gospel
Sermon	Sermon
Creed	Creed
Intercessions	Prayers
Hymn and collection	Hymn and collection
Reading 1 Cor. 11.23-26	Reading 1 Cor. 11.23-26
	Verses
	Humble access
Invitation to confession	
General confession	Confession
1 John 2.1-2	1 John 2.1-2
Uncovering the consecrated bread and wine	Uncovering the consecrated bread and wine
(Lord's Prayer)	(Lord's Prayer)
Silence	Silence
	Invitation
Communion	Communion
Sentence	Sentence
Concluding prayers	Concluding prayers
Grace or ending prayer	Grace or ending prayer

THE CHURCH OF THE PROVINCE OF NEW ZEALAND 1989[1]
The *New Zealand Service Book* includes 'A Service of Holy Communion'[2] and 'A Service of the Word with Holy Communion.'[3] These services are used in the rural parts of the Province where one priest may have charge of a number of small congregations. The service may be conducted by a deacon or a reader. Readers automatically receive the required permission as a part of their licensing.

A New Zealand Prayer Book 1989
A Service of the Word with Holy Communion
Any eucharistic liturgy up to 'The Affirmation of Faith'
The Prayers of the People' excluding the Lord's prayer
Thanksgiving (see Text 8)
The peace
Optional prayer (see Text 9)
Invitation
Communion
'Prayer after communion' including the Lord's prayer but not the blessing

The rite includes a thanksgiving prayer (Text 8). This is an addition to the intercessions and makes no specific reference to the elements, save to thanks God generally for the sacrament. There is an optional prayer, said before communion (Text 9), which links the receiving and sending congregations. An earlier version of this service for use with the 1984 liturgies was authorized by the then Bishop of Dunedin for his diocese.[4] However, the development of 'community priests' may lead to declining use of this service in New Zealand.

OBSERVATIONS
The gradual adoption of the practice of extended communion in the Anglican Communion seems to have been with little initial reflection. The modern provision seem to be the result of two forces; firstly the growth of the parish communion and the centrality of the eucharist, secondly the difficulty of providing clergy in the rural areas. It is to be noted that even in Provinces that have women priests (e.g. Canada), provision for extended communion still exists.

---

[1] Since 1992 entitled 'Anglican Church in Aotearoa, New Zealand and Polynesia'.
[2] Church of the Province of New Zealand, *A New Zealand Prayer Book* (Collins, Auckland, 1989) pp.729-737.
[3] *ibid.*, pp.518-520.
[4] B. Peters, *The Anglican Eucharist in New Zealand 1814-1989* (Alcuin/GROW Joint Liturgical Study 21, Grove Books, Bramcote, 1992), pp.36-40; also see *'Leading Anglican Worship' A Guide for Lay Readers, Kai Karakia, officiants and the newly ordained* [nd, no publisher or author], pp.16-21.

6. The British Isles

Extended communion is unknown in the Church of Ireland, but is sanctioned in both the Church in Wales and the Episcopal Church of Scotland. The Church of England is in a more complex position with the House of Bishops discouraging the practice while some dioceses give their approval.[1] Thus individual diocesan regulations will have to be examined. But first comes the Second Table Service of the Church of Scotland, for here is an order of extended communion within Presbyterianism.

THE CHURCH OF SCOTLAND 1940

In the *Book of Common Order* 1940 is a service for the Second Table, a variation on the Short Order of Holy Communion.

Book of Common Order 1940	
Short Order	Second Table
Psalm/hymn	
Call to Prayer	
Collect of purity	
Confession	
Prayer of forgiveness	
Short lessons	
Apostles Creed	
Sermon (if any)	
Communion hymn	
Words of Institution	
Taking	Explanation
Eucharistic Prayer	
Sursum Corda	Gracious words
Preface	
Sanctus	
anamnesis	Invitation
epiclesis	
self-oblation	
intercessions	Prayer
doxology	(for fruitful communion)
Lord's prayer	
Fraction	
Communion	
Thanksgiving	
Psalm/hymn	
Benediction	

[1] In November 1993 a report was brought to General Synod which included possible texts.

The context is that of infrequent celebration of communion with services of preparation and special preaching. Tables were laid with communicants sitting around to eat. With large numbers of communicants it was not possible for all to partake at one sitting. One solution would be to have a number of celebrations, but a high view of the sacrament allowed the Second Table from that previously consecrated. This is clearly stated in the explanation,

'Beloved in the Lord; you see before you, on the Holy Table, the bread and the wine which have already this day been set apart from all common uses unto this holy use and mystery; and have been sanctified by the Word of God and prayer.'[1]

The prayer for fruitful communion has an epiclesis upon the communicants. It may seem remarkable that the Church of Scotland should have authorized this service, but the introduction to the Book says, 'without reservation of any kind it may be asserted that everything contained in this book receives its warrant from that source [Holy Scripture]'.[2] It would appear that this service has died out with the growth of more frequent communion.

THE CHURCH IN WALES 1974

Wales licenses deacons as vicars, requiring provision for extended communion. The General Directions in the 1984 traditional language communion service say 'A Deacon may administer Holy Communion from the reserved Sacrament',[3] for the Welsh bishops had approved in 1974 an *Order for Public Administration of Holy Communion from the Reserved Sacrament by a Deacon* (Text 10).

This is a simple provision; there are only a few parishes where deacons are incumbent. If this became more widespread, it is to be hoped that a fuller examination of the liturgical provision could be made. With deacon incumbents questions arise about the procurement of the sacrament. Sometimes a neighbouring priest may come in and preside at the eucharist, but for practical reasons this is most likely to be mid-week. Alternatively the deacon may attend a eucharist in a neighbouring parish collecting the sacrament to take back to the parish. The result of this is that the Sunday eucharist may become a very infrequent event in the worship of that parish. As one of the sacraments is administered but not celebrated, what are the ecclesiological consequences? Article XIX sees two marks of the visible church, 'the pure word of God is preached' and 'the sacraments be duly ministered according to Christ's ordinance'. Extended communion is not a eucharist; there is no taking bread and giving thanks. In the sense of the article has the parish has ceased to do 'all those things that of necessity are requisite to the same'?

THE SCOTTISH EPISCOPAL CHURCH 1992

An experimental rite for extended communion services led by deacons and lay persons was authorized in 1992 for a period of five years. One notable feature is

---

[1] *Book of Common Order* (OUP, Glasgow, 1940), p.132.
[2] *ibid.*, p.(v).
[3] C. O. Buchanan (ed.), *Latest Anglican Liturgies* (SPCK, Grove Books, London, 1985), p.72.

the three thanksgiving prayers. The first is said to be 'from the Deacon's Proclamation Liturgy of Addai and Mari' (Text 12), the second is based on a French prayer, and the third for use with the 1970 liturgy is the General Thanksgiving. The service at the altar has words of explanation (Text 11) which inform the congregation at which church the elements were consecrated.

Communion 1992
Service of the Word
concluding with alms
Prepare consecrated elements
Words of explanation (Text 11)
Thanksgiving Prayer (3 forms)
Lord's Prayer (and humble access)
Communion
Ablutions
Post communion prayer
(doxology)
Dismissal

The Episcopal Church has for many years been willing to communicate from the reserved sacrament. The rubrics of the 1912 *Book of Common Prayer* said,
> 'According to the long existing custom in the Scottish Church, the Presbyter may reserve so much of the Consecrated Gift as may be required for the communion of the sick, and others who could not be present at the celebration in church.'[1]

Thus the church has developed a rite which gives shape to this earlier permission.

THE CHURCH OF ENGLAND

All sorts of experiments have occurred in the Church of England. This is in part due to the rise of a large number of women deacons, but also due to the licensing of laity to administer the sacrament in church, and the provision of extended communion to the sick in *Ministry to the Sick* 1983 (Text 13). The House of Bishops discussed the issue in 1982, 1989 and 1993, producing a confidential policy.[2] There is great variation of implementation of this from one diocese to another.[3] Stories circulate of various practices, including the whole congregation repeating the eucharistic prayer together (to remind them what has already occurred), and selected parts of the eucharistic prayer being said (often the preface, but sometimes everything but the narrative of institution). *Faith in the Countryside*[4] has asked for further

---

[1] *Book of Common Prayer* (CUP, Edinburgh, 1912), p.284.
[2] See *News of Liturgy*, No. 217 (Jan. 1993), p.3.
[3] G. Jeanes, 'Communion by Extension' in *News of Liturgy*, No. 205 (Jan. 1992).
[4] Archbishop's Commission on Rural Areas, *Faith in the Countryside* (Churchman, 1990), p.190.

discussion, as does *Deacons Now*.[1] Many dioceses actively discourage the practice, but some have produced their own regulations[2] and others liturgical materials. The House of Bishops introduced a report to General Synod in 1993 for a 'take note' debate to find the mind of the church. This report included a draft liturgy.[3] The debate revealed a much more widespread interest in lay presidency of the eucharist than had previously been suspected. The liturgical text was not at that point being introduced into Synod for authorization.

(a) Carlisle 1979, 1990

David Smethurst reported on the situation in Carlisle.[4] The diocesan regulations of 1979 were tightened in the Easter 1990 *Ad Clerum*. While welcoming extension to the sick and housebound the bishop does not approve of extension for house groups or for a Sunday services. He does not discuss old people's homes or day centres. On Sunday the bishop rightly sees the priority being that of a eucharist by an episcopally ordained priest. There is even a direct quote from the House of Bishops:

> 'Because the total eucharistic action of priest and people, including the Consecration of the Elements, should be a single, indivisible whole, the House of Bishops disapproves of the use of Extended Communion as a means whereby a congregation can receive the sacrament in church in the absence of the parish priest.'[5]

Thus the cautious policy in 1979 was replaced with a more restricted one in 1990, which left only Ulverston continuing the previous practice.

(b) Religious [nd]

Women's religious communities are a distinct category. With the ordination of women as deaconesses and deacons, so came the possibility of communion from the reserved sacrament. One particular community had a prayer 'authorized' by their bishop. (Text 13). The service is basically ASB, the thanksgiving prayer adapting the first eucharistic prayer.

(c) Coventry 1991

The regulations of Coventry cover theology, rules of practice and liturgy. The theological section emphasizes that we are 'joined in one action' against concentrating on 'mechanistic or magical ideas' to do with the elements. The rules make sure that there is a monthly communion in the 'receiving' place. The words from Ministry to the Sick (Text 14) are used after the placing of the elements, and then follows the Lord's Prayer as in the ASB.

---

[1] ACCM, *Deacons Now* (Ludo Press, London, 1991) p.69.
[2] Diocese of Oxford, *Oxford Diocesan Year Book 1992* (Oxford Diocesan Publications Ltd., 1992), p.241.
[3] General Synod of the Church of England, *Extended Communion. A Report by the House of Bishops* (GS 1082, June, 1993).
[4] D. Smethurst, *Extended Communion: An Experiment in Cumbria* (Grove Books, Bramcote, 1986).
[5] Bishop of Carlisle, *Ad Clerum* (Easter 1990), p.2.

(d) Durham 1991

Durham Diocesan Liturgical Committee produced a service of extended communion for use by deacons.[1] The service, following the ASB, begins with an expanded version of the explanation from *Ministry to the Sick* (§10). After the peace, a member of the congregation reads a lesson with strong eucharistic implications (four choices are given, one being 1 Cor. 11.23-29). The collect of Maundy Thursday is followed by verses from Ps. 116 which give a flavour of praise. Then comes the Lord's Prayer and communion. This service shows the need, both to provide a reading that links what we are doing to that of scripture, and for some thanks and praise.

(e) Salisbury 1991

Salisbury has 'authorized' a series of booklets of Extended Communion, variations on Rite A, Rite B and the Book of Common Prayer.

Extended Communion—Salisbury		
Rite A	Rite B	BCP 1662
Preparation		
Hymn	Hymn	Hymn
Welcome	Welcome	Lord's prayer
Collect for purity	Collect for purity	Collect for purity
Penitence —invitation —confession —absolution		
Kyrie	Kyrie or 10 commandments or summary of the law	Kyrie or summary of the law
Gloria	Gloria	
		Collect for the Queen
Collect of the day	Collect of the day	Collect of the day
Ministry of the Word		
OT/NT	OT/NT	Epistle
Hymn	Hymn	Hymn
Gospel	Gospel	Gospel
Sermon	Sermon	Creed
Creed	Creed	Sermon
Collection	Collection	Collection

---

[1] G. Jeanes, *op. cit.*, pp.5-8.

	The Prayers		
Intercessions	Intercessions	Prayer for Church militant
(Penitence	Comfortable words	
—invitation	Invitation	Invitation
—confession	confession	confession
—absolution)	absolution	absolution
		comfortable words
	Act of Thanksgiving		
Invitation	Invitation	Invitation
General Thanksgiving	General Thanksgiving	General Thanksgiving
	Ministry of the Sacrament		
Explanation	Explanation	Explanation
Humble Access	Humble Access	Humble Access
Peace	Peace	
Hymn	Hymn	Hymn
	The Communion		
Lord's Prayer	Lord's Prayer	
Agnus Dei	Agnus Dei	
Invitation	Invitation	
Communion	Communion	Communion
	After Communion		
After Communion	After Communion	After Communion
Sentence	Sentence	Lord's prayer
Thanksgiving	Thanksgiving	Thanksgiving
		Gloria
Dismissal	Dismissal	Dismissal

The outer cover makes clear that this is a service of extended communion 'for use where the consecrated gifts are taken from one church for use in another church.'[1] The notes direct the minister to lead from the lectern and only to go to the holy table for the distribution. Also the collection is taken after the creed to avoid the consecrated elements becoming a part of an offertory procession.

---

[1] Diocese of Salisbury, *Extended Communion According to the use of the Alternative Service Book Rite 'A'*, front cover.

Otherwise the service proceeds as in the ASB until before the prayer of humble access. Two additions are made at this point. Firstly comes an act of thanksgiving, then comes a reading of the Last Supper and an exhortation which explains the context. The service continues omitting the eucharistic prayer and the fraction. This is a very carefully thought out rite and has skilfully avoided many difficulties. The one weakness is the minimal seasonal provision.

(f) St Edmundsbury and Ipswich 1992
Diocesan regulations require that during the intercessions the church where the elements were consecrated must be included. Instead of the eucharistic prayer a number of suggestions are made: firstly a devotion using the 'Father of all' prayer (ASB §52); secondly, a reading from scripture that includes the institution of the Lord's Supper; thirdly prayers in the communion of the sick; fourthly Good Friday devotions; fifthly traditional elements from the eucharistic rite, Sursum Corda, Sanctus and Agnus Dei. Such freedom is allowed but 'it must be clear to the congregation that what is taking place is not the consecration of the elements'.

(g) Hereford 1993
There are suggestions for how to send out the consecrated bread and wine. At the receiving church the minister has to announce that the elements have been consecrated elsewhere, naming the place, either after the sermon (for BCP services) or after the presentation of the offerings (ASB). In both rites the procedure is to omit anything to do with the eucharistic prayer.

OBSERVATIONS
Although Wales and Scotland have made provision for extended communion, England seems to be in a muddle. Of the diocesan provision Durham and Sarum are particularly commendable. They both want to connect the service with the Last Supper through a reading of suitable verses. They both have thanksgiving material. As context clarifies the difference between extended communion and the eucharist, the directions about where the minister is to sit take on particular importance. These can reinforce or undermine the distinction between the two services; as can the use (or not) of a distinct service booklet.

There are a number of pastoral problems with extended communion. One is the relationship of the priest and people. A sharp division between president and pastoral care is made, if a church ceases to have the vicar lead Holy Communions. Thus, if extended communion becomes common in a parish, it is desirable that particular churches do not become permanent satellites, but rather that the location of the main eucharist and the satellite celebration should be frequently changed.

7. Theological Issues

A number of objections have been raised against the practice of communion out-side the eucharist. Jerome spoke of the difficulty of keeping church discipline with home communion. In Anglicanism there have been questions, both about the wisdom of the practice compared to alternate pastoral strategies, and questions on the theological level.[1] While the authorities in the Catholic church seem to be pointing towards an expansion of eucharistic services, theologians and liturgists are uneasy. This chapter looks at the discussion based around these headings: strategies, eucharist and communion, consecration, and thanksgiving. No conclusions can as yet be reached because the matters are still under debate.

STRATEGIES

Anglicans have in many parts of the world adopted the pattern of a weekly eucharist, which is now proving difficult to sustain. This seems to leave them to four different possible strategies. Firstly, ordain larger numbers of priests, a growing number being non-stipendiary, and even 'locally' licensed. Secondly, provide regulations for extended communion. Thirdly, authorize some form of 'lay presidency'. Fourthly, abandon the weekly Sunday eucharist.

Lay presidency is practised in some Free Churches. It came very close to being part of the policy of the Province of the Southern Cone.[2] It seems that Bishop Hanson wanted this to be discussed rather than the 'unsatisfactory' practice of extended communion.[3] Robin Nixon suggested it is the answer both during an interregnum and for clergy who look after more than one congregation.[4] While some Anglicans are willing to consider the possibility, there is a very frosty reaction by others. 'There is no historical precedent for this within our church . . . other more satisfactory ways must be found,' says the Archbishop of Brisbane.[5] ACC-7, though not very encouraging of extended communion, was also discouraging of lay presidency, 'ACC-6 was convinced that the Anglican tradition of priests presiding at the Eucharist should be upheld . . . we endorse the previous view'.[6] Thus, although there has been growing support for the idea in evangelical circles[7], they have been unable to sway the rest of Anglicanism, which prefers the other options.

---

[1] *A Report to the Archbishop of Melbourne, op. cit.,* pp.2-5, and R. Beckwith, 'Extended Communion: One Parish's Experience. A Response' in *Churchman,* Vol. 100 (1986) pp.335-338.
[2] A. Hargrave, *But Who will Preside?* (Grove Worship Series No. 113, Grove Books, Bramcote, 1990).
[3] Bp. R. Hanson, 'Extended Communion Unsatisfactory', letter to *Church Times* (28 Dec. 1979).
[4] R. Nixon, 'Some Theological issues in Favour' in *Lay presidency at the Eucharist?* T. Lloyd (ed.) (Grove Liturgical Studies No. 9, Grove Books, Bramcote, 1977), pp. 26-32.
[5] *Ad Clerum* (28 July 1992).
[6] *Many Gifts One Spirit,* ACC-7 (Church House Publishing, London, 1987), p.57.
[7] C. J. Cocksworth, *Evangelical Eucharistic Thought in the Church of England* (CUP, Cambridge, 1993), pp.168-170.

EUCHARIST AND COMMUNION SERVICE
One of the sharpest problems and points of attack on services of extended communion is in the relationship between the eucharist and the later communion service. A variety of approaches and metaphors have been used to explain the link. Basil the Great suggested that the home communicant 'must believe that he duly takes and receives it from the hand that first gave it . . . it comes to the same thing, whether one or many portions are received from the priest'.[1] Few people today advocate such a view, for no one is proposing home communion, but Hatchett did see this as the background to the ECUSA BCP 1979 services, and commented that the early church's approach was,
'an anamnesis of the last eucharistic assembly which spoke of Sunday as the first day of the week and all which that represented, and a foretaste of the next eucharistic assembly which represented Sunday as the 'eighth day' and all which that signified.'[2]
But this relates to home communion in the context of a Sunday eucharist rather than a main service by extension.
A variety of metaphors have been used to signify the relationship. Colin Buchanan has talked of 'main celebration' and 'satellite events'.[3] The regulations have often tried to avoid this becoming an established one-way relationship. Canon Wendel proposed the party cake image, which links it to an example of 'secular' extension and celebration.[4] This gives a model for how celebrations can be connected and of oneness. Liturgically, this has received expression by: introductory explanations (Catholic Apostolic), notices (*Sunday Celebrations*, Durham), and through intercessions (St. Edmundsbury and Ipswich). Most of these seem to do less than justice to celebration theory. Presbyterians talked of a 'second table'; communion being open to those who were unable to feast earlier. Thus the service is seen as a banquet in which there are two sittings for the same meal.
Coventry saw extension as 'joined in one action', another viewpoint on extended communion. The provisions note that Dix developed the fourfold shape theory of eucharistic actions; taking, thanking, breaking, receiving. Rather than look at the communion as a separated action, Coventry stresses the unity of the actions: The second congregation is seen as joined in the one eucharistic action. Implicit questions are: What are the criteria for constituting a local church? Is it when two or three are gathered together? More often in people's minds it is to do with the possession of a building. Or is it a place where the word is preached and the sacraments are administered? If so, is the eucharistic community the local church? In which case it is fundamentally tied with ministers of the sacrament, in Anglicanism with the provision of priests, making the position of a 'deacon in charge' problematical. Is the basic unit where communion is administered, or where the eucharist is celebrated? Anglican tradition suggests the latter.

---

[1] W. H. Freestone, *op. cit.*, p.41.
[2] M. J. Hatchett, *op. cit.*, p.409.
[3] D. Smethurst, *op. cit.*, p.17.
[4] C. P. Price, *op. cit.*, p.86.

CONSECRATION

Underlying any form of extended communion is some concept of consecration. This may not be immediately apparent in some liturgical texts but it is in others. The Byzantine cry out, 'Holy Presanctified things for the holy'.[1] The East Syrian liturgy of the Signing of the Chalice was clear about the previous consecration:

'they have been hallowed and completed and perfected by the brooding of the Holy Ghost, and the bread by his working has become the living Body, which was given for the life of the world, and the wine by his operation your blood of the New Testament,'

and about the desire for the placing of the holy bread into the wine to be a consecratory action:

'we sign this chalice with your Body . . . that as by the wound of the spear blood came forth from your side, so also now by your will may this mixture be perfected by the might of your Body, so as to become your propitiatory Blood.'[2]

The Roman rite has a doctrine of consecration based on a validly ordained priest reciting the words of institution. This may be seen as going back at least to the time of Ambrose,

'Before it is consecrated it is bread; but when the words of Christ have been uttered over it, it is the body of Christ . . . And the chalice, before the words of Christ, it is full of wine and water. But when the words of Christ have done their work, it becomes the blood of Christ which has redeemed the people.'[3]

So there are careful directions to ensure that no confusion is made between a eucharistic service and the Mass.

The opening statement of the Church of Scotland Second Table service says:

'you see before you, on the Holy Table, the bread and the wine which have been already this day set apart from all common use unto this holy use and mystery; and which have been sanctified by the Word of God and prayer to be for us the Communion . . .'[4]

Here consecration is tied to 1 Timothy 4.4-5, which has been the position of the Reformed rite as found in the *Westminster Directory* and others.[5] This therefore excludes an epiclesis on the elements, rather we have one on the people, 'vouchsafe to bless with Thy Holy Spirit us Thy servants here before Thee' by a fruitful reception.[6]

---

[1] Ryan and J. de Uinck, *op. cit.*,p.383.

[2] H. W. Codrington, 'The Syrian liturgies of the Presanctified III East Syrian or Persian', *op. cit.*, p.541.

[3] E. Yarnold, *The Awe Inspiring Rites of Initiation* (St. Paul Publications, Slough, 1971), pp.137-138.

[4] *Book of Common Order* (1940), *op. cit.*, p.123.

[5] *The Westminster Directory* (Grove Liturgical Study No. 21, Grove Books, Bramcote, 1980), p.23; see also D. Kennedy and P. Tovey, *Methodist and United Reformed Church Worship* (Grove Worship Series No. 120, (Grove Books, Bramcote, 1992), pp.24-25.

[6] *Book of Common Order* (1940), *op. cit.*, p.133.

The modern Anglican view of consecration is articulated in the Commentary on the ASB

'The Eucharistic prayer is not called in the rite "The Prayer of Consecration", but it is still viewed as "consecrating" ... there is now no solemnly identified formula or "moment of consecration". Rather, the whole giving of thanks sets the theological context within which we can confidently assert that this *is* the communion of the body and blood of the Lord.'[1]

This is in line with Moscow Agreed Statement:

'The consecration of the bread and wine results from the whole sacramental liturgy. The act of consecration includes certain proper and appropriate moments—thanksgiving, anamnesis, *Epiclesis*. The deepest understanding rejects any consecration by formula.'[2]

There would however appear to be diversity (confusion?) within Anglicanism as to the effects of consecration.[3] Such questions also arose in the ARCIC discussions which concluded:

'According to the traditional order of the liturgy the consecratory prayer (*anaphora*) leads to the communion of the faithful. Through this prayer of thanksgiving, a word of faith addressed to the Father, the bread and the wine become the body and blood of Christ by the action of the Holy Spirit.'[4]

They went on to consider reservation with some comments very pertinent to extended communion:

'communion administered from the reserved sacrament to those unable to attend the eucharistic celebration is rightly understood as an extension of that celebration.'[5]

Again some Anglicans have been uneasy with this:

'This excludes the historic teaching of the Church of England ... that the presence of Christ's body and blood is only in the reception of them.'[6]

But not all would agree that this sort of receptionism is the position of the Prayer Book and the Articles.[7] Individual doctrines of consecration will influence the reaction to extended communion, and its implicit 'stronger' approach.

Paul Avis in his review of ACORA, the 'Countryside' report which called for a reconsideration of the episcopal disapproval of communion by extension, threw out the objection:

'What is the theological justification for extended communion, which separates the offering from the reception of the sacrament?'[8]

---

[1] *The Alternative Service Book 1980. A Commentary by the Liturgical Commission* (CIO, London, 1980) pp.78-79.

[2] *Anglican—Orthodox Dialogue* (SPCK, London, 1984), p.57.

[3] C. J. Cocksworth, *op. cit.*, p.148.

[4] ARCIC, *The Final Report* (CTS/SPCK, London, 1982), pp.15-16.

[5] *ibid.*, p.23.

[6] R. T. Beckwith, *Rome and Canterbury the Final ARCIC Report* (Latimer House, Oxford, 1982) p.15.

[7] R. Buxton, *op. cit.*

[8] P. Avis, 'Review Article. Faith and Fantasy in the Countryside' in *Theology*, Vol. XCIV No. 758 (March/April 1991), p.128; see also P. Avis, 'Extended Communion: the case against it' in *Church Times* (10 Sept. 1993), p.10.

A parallel objection comes from Gerard Austin with regard to the epiclesis: 'eucharistic reality is about a conversion: not only of the elements of bread and wine but of the gathered assembly of the baptized.'[1] He sees these two aspects of the epiclesis as intimately connected (and so argues for a united epiclesis) seeing them as sundered in rites for extended communion. Again we are back to the question: Can we have a united eucharistic action divided between different congregations? The various rites of the churches and ARCIC would seem to say 'yes', based on their views of consecration. Avis and Austin give warnings of possible dangers 'that this 'is to impoverish our liturgical tradition, and to rob Sunday, the day of the Lord, of its paschal significance.'[2]

THANKSGIVING
Services of extended communion have varied in their inclusion (or not) of thanksgiving. The underlying question is: when is a thanksgiving a eucharist? The *Vatican Directory* said:
'This thanksgiving should not in any way take the form of a Eucharistic prayer, to avoid the danger of confusion. The texts of the preface and the Eucharistic Prayer ... must not be used.'[3]
It is however the Roman Catholics, who, within this constraint, have been the most generous in the provision of thanksgiving prayers for such rites.
Anglicans seem to have a general paucity of thanksgiving in their liturgy when compared to other traditions.[4] Their position of consecration by thanksgiving might make them cautious. But in the process of liturgical revision, and in ecumenical dialogue, the question of the content of a full eucharistic prayer has been faced and answered. The 1965 Pan-Anglican Document states:
'The consecration prayer should be in the form of a thanksgiving for creation and for God's mighty acts in Christ and in the sending of the Holy Spirit. There should be a recital of the words and acts of the Lord at the Last Supper and a prayer for the communicants.'[5]
This Anglican minimum creates boundaries between a thanksgiving and a consecratory eucharistic prayer. *BEM* gave guidelines on a eucharistic prayer, expanding the suggestions above to include an anamnesis and epiclesis. It also seemed to approve of reserving the elements for those who are sick 'and those who are absent'.[6] In Anglicanism similarly these components are usually seen as essential to a eucharistic prayer, again giving clarity to distinctions between different types of thanksgiving. However it is noticeable that while eastern liturgies of the presanctified are of office and communion, modern rites are adaptations of the eucharistic liturgy. Perhaps the older tradition makes a clearer distinction that 'this service is not a eucharist' than much contemporary liturgy.

[1] G. Austin, 'Communion Services: A Break with Tradition?' in G. Austin (ed.) *Fountain of Life*, (Pastoral Press, Washington, 1991), p.210.
[2] *ibid.*, p.211.
[3] Directory on Sunday Celebrations in the Absence of a Priest, §45.
[4] P. Tovey, 'Sedro and General Thanksgiving' in *The Harp*, Vol. III No. 1 & 2 (June 1990) pp.67-74.
[5] C. O. Buchanan (ed.), *Modern Anglican Liturgies 1958-1968* (OUP, Oxford, 1968), p.32.
[6] WCC, *Baptism Eucharist and Ministry* (Geneva 1982), p.17.

8. Postscript

This study of communion outside of the eucharist has revealed great variety in practice. A wide range of factors that have given rise to such services. It would seem that the practice will continue not only in the Liturgies of the Presanctified but also in the more modern rites of extended communion. Indeed it looks as if this may become the regular Sunday fare for the faithful of the Roman Catholic church.

Ancient home communion has died out, yet it is used to justify many of the succeeding forms of communion. Liturgies of the Presanctified continue in the Byzantine tradition, and survive in the Maronite church. Maybe the liturgical revival in the Syro-Malabar church will lead to its restitution in that community. The western form has undergone a resurrection in many Anglican Provinces.

Modern rites of extended communion in part stem back to the Tridentine rite. Their appearance in Anglicanism seems to be a parallel development. Although Graff made a distinction between Communion outside the Mass and Eucharistic Services, there is a clear development of the modern forms from the Tridentine rite. In some ways these rites build on the monastic tradition, corporate, lay, and simple, but parish usage is leading to their elaboration.

Different contexts have led to communion (i.e. distribution of communion) services. Presently the growing shortage of priests, or their inability to celebrate regularly in small scattered Christian communities, is encouraging these services. The new-found role of the laity in the administration of communion has also been a factor. Proponents admit that it is most appropriate that the Sunday Service be a eucharist, and extended communion is second best. But it would appear that pastoral factors override, and the church is likely to continue to need these services in the future. Ordaining women to the priesthood does not necessarily fill the gap. Probably only the provision of local priests will resolve the problem.

9. Texts

SUNDAY CELEBRATIONS 1976 1978

Sunday Celebrations ICEL, (Washington, 1978), is the English translation of *Assemblée dominicales en l'absence du prêtre* from the Le Centre National de Pastorale Liturgique, Paris. The first extract is *Prayer of Praise and Thanksgiving A* (pp 24-25) one of four thanksgivings that occur between the intercessions and the rite of communion. The second extract is the first of two 'words of invitation' (p31) which comes from the rite of communion between the Lord's Prayer and 'This is the Lamb of God ...'

TEXT 1

We give you thanks, Lord our God,
for this world which you have given us.
You never cease to renew it,
and through the work of our hands
you seek to make it better.

All: **Glory to God in the Highest!**

You have made all people in your image.
Each of us is made in your likeness,
with the ability to recognize the outline of your face
in the lives of all our brothers and sisters.

All: **Glory to God in the Highest!**

You did not want to be distant from us,
and so you taught us to recognize you
through the words of Moses and the prophets,
who told us the wonderful story of your love.

All: **Glory to God in the Highest!**

But you came even closer to us through your Son, Jesus Christ.
In him, you walked through our streets,
you looked upon us with human eyes
and in many ways lived like us
creating the joy of unforgettable encounters.

All: **Glory to God in the Highest!**

Through the death and resurrection of your Son,
you drew us into the intimacy of your life,
so that today, when we live in him,
we live in you through the Holy Spirit,
your gift to us.

All: **Glory to God in the Highest!**

And so, with all our fellow Christians in the world
who are joined together today,
and in the company of all the saints,
we pray to you, as brothers and sisters:

All: **Our Father ...**

TEXT 2

A word of invitation expressing the connection between this communion and the celebration of the Mass should always be mentioned. For example, the leader may say:

A Today our pastor (Father *N.*) is celebrating the eucharist at *N.* We are united with him and with those who are participating in the Mass that is being celebrated. By receiving the bread consecrated at the last Mass celebrated here, we too share in the body of Christ and are united in his sacrifice.

RITUAL FOR LAY PRESIDERS 1984

Ritual for Lay Presiders (Western Liturgical Conference, St. Peter's Press, Saskatchewan, 1984) includes 8 Thanksgiving Prayers, the following being the first (pp.9-12). It also includes two 'admonitions to unity' (p.15) immediately after the peace; the text below is the first of these.

TEXT 3

We praise you and thank you, Father of all. We praise you and thank you for sharing with us, your children, the gift of life. All life comes from you, Father, and all life returns to you. We praise you and thank you and bless you, for the gift of all gifts, Jesus our Lord. We thank you, Father!

All: **Praise to you, Lord, King of eternal glory.**
Or: **Glory and praise to you, O Lord Jesus Christ.**

We thank you for calling us into your family through Jesus, who is the Good News of our salvation. We thank you for accepting the gift of Jesus' surrender, for raising him from the dead by the power of your Holy Spirit, for making him Lord of all creation, the eternal high priest who pleads our cause at your right hand. We thank you, Father!

All: **Praise to you, Lord, King of eternal glory.**

We thank you for the gift of the Eucharist, for the coming of your Son Jesus among us: one Lord, one holy bread of life, one holy and ever glorious body. By our communion in Christ, we are united with the whole Church. You make the salvation Jesus gained for us present here and now, as it was in the Upper Room, at the Last Supper, and as it was at Calvary, when we passed over to you and was glorified.

Jesus is our altar, our eternal high priest; He is the head of his body, the Church. He is our perfect gift to you, O Father!

All: **Praise to you, Lord, King of eternal glory.**

We praise you for calling us into the one, holy, catholic Church of your Son. We pray in union with the virgin Mary the all-holy mother of God, and with Joseph, her husband.

Unite us in prayer with the holy Apostles Peter and Paul, and all your martyrs and saints.

All: **Praise to you, Lord, King of eternal glory.**

We ask your mercy upon all who have died, those of our own families, and all who have called upon Jesus in faith. May they find light and happiness with Christ Jesus the Lord, and a blessed peace at the last.

All: **Praise to you, Lord, King of eternal glory.**

TEXT 4

The auxiliary minister, from time to time, will declare the unity of this community with the whole Church, in these or similar words:
Holy Communion is the sign of our membership in the Church, the Body of Christ. We are now invited to be in special union with N., our pastor. In this holy communion, we share in the Eucharist which is offered for our good, and for the good of the whole world.

DUNKELD SCOTLAND 1764
F. C. Eeles reports in *Traditional Ceremonial and Customs connected with the Scottish Liturgy* (Alcuin Club Collection XVII, Longmans Green & Co., 1910) pp.92-93, that in the copy of the Scottish Liturgy used by Bishop Alexander of Dunkeld between 1764 and 1776 a long prayer is added in manuscript, to be said in place of the consecration, when communion was given with the reserved Sacrament.

TEXT 5

When the consecrated elements are reserved, and a new company is afterwards to be communicated of them, the following may be used instead of the Consecration Prayer:
Almighty God our heavenly Father, who of thy tender mercy didst give thine only Son J. + C. to suffer death upon the cross for our redemption, who made there by his own oblation of himself once offered, a full, perfect and sufficient sacrifice, oblation, and satisfaction for the sins of the whole world, and did institute, and in his holy Gospel command us to continue, a perpetual memorial of that his precious death and sacrifice until his coming again; hear us, O merciful Father, we most humbly beseech thee, and of they almighty goodness vouchsafe so to bless with thy Holy Spirit us (these) thy servants here before thee, and to grant that we (they) receiving thy gifts and creatures of bread and wine already consecrated into the most precious body and blood of they Son our Saviour J. + C according to his holy institution, and in commemoration of his death and passion, may be made partakers of all the benefits of the same: and so sanctify our (their) whole spirits, souls, and bodies, that we (they) may become holy, living, and acceptable sacrifices unto thee. And we entirely desire thy Fatherly goodness to be propitious to us sinners: and grant that by the merits and death of thy Son, and through faith in his blood, we and all thy whole Church may obtain remission of our sins, may be delivered from the Devil and his snares, may be fulfilled with thy grace and heavenly benediction, and be made one body with him, that he may dwell in us, and we in him, and at the last may obtain everlasting life with thee; thou, O Lord Almighty, being through him reconciled unto us, and by whom and with whom, in the unity of the Holy Ghost, all honour and glory be unto thee, O Father Almighty, world without end. Amen.

The following is the introductory address for a service of communion outside the eucharist; from *The Liturgy and other Divine Offices of the Church* (George J. W. Pitman, London, 1892) pp.25-26.

TEXT 6

THE ORDER
FOR THE
ADMINISTRATION OF THE COMMUNION
ON THE AFTERNOON OF THE LORD'S DAY
TO THOSE WHO WERE NOT PRESENT
AT THE CONSECRATION.

The Priest standing at the access to the sanctuary shall address those present as follows

Dearly beloved in the Lord, Ye see before you the bread which hath been broken, and the cup which hath been blessed, in the Church of God, and which as the apostle saith, are the Communion of the Body and of the Blood of Christ. And Almighty God, who is full of tenderness towards the necessities o f His creatures, hath ordained this holy service, that you, who were hindered from approaching to His holy table in the morning, but who were present in your desires and in the unity of the Holy Ghost, as sheep of the fold of Jesus Christ and faithful members of this flock, may now be blessed in partaking of this heavenly feast.

Remember, I beseech you, the holy act which hath been wrought in the service of this day. These creatures of bread and wine brought up by His congregation, have been accepted of God; and through the operation of the Holy Ghost, by the word of God and by prayer, have been made unto His Church the Flesh and Blood of Jesus Christ. And being thus sanctified, they have been presented before God, in memorial of that one Sacrifice upon the cross once offered by Jesus Christ, full, perfect, and sufficient; for the sake whereof the mercy of God hath been besought on behalf of all God's Church and people, for you, and for all men, even the remission of all our sins, and everlasting life.

Of this bread and this cup your brethren have partaken, feeding on that Flesh, and drinking that Blood: and now, in the Name of God, and of our Lord Jesus Christ, I invite you also, as being one with them in the communion of the Holy Ghost, to draw near and partake thereof.
And as it becomes us at all times to confess our sins, and cast ourselves upon the mercy of God, waiting for His forgiveness; so especially at this time it becomes us to humble ourselves before Him, in thus coming into His immediate presence, and seeking this blessing at His hands. Wherefore I beseech you to accompany me with all your heart, making your humble confession unto Almighty God, meekly kneeling upon your knees.

ECUSA 1979
The following are the rubrics found in *The Book of Common Prayer* (The Church Hymnal Corporation and The Seabury Press, 1979) pp.408-409.

TEXT 7
When the services of a priest cannot be obtained, the bishop may, at discretion, authorize a deacon to distribute Holy Communion to the congregation from the reserved Sacrament in the following manner:

1. *After the Liturgy of the Word (and the receiving of the people's offering), the deacon reverently places the consecrated Sacrament on the Altar, during which time a communion hymn may be sung.*
2. *The Lord's Prayer is then said, the deacon first saying, 'Let us pray in the words our Saviour Christ hath (has) taught us.'*
3. *And then, omitting the breaking of the Bread, the deacon proceeds with what follows in the liturgy as far as the end of the postcommunion prayer, and then dismisses the people.*

If any of the consecrated Bread or Wine remain, apart from any which may be required for the Communion of the sick, or of others who for weighty cause could not be present at the celebration, or for the administration of Communion by a deacon to a congregation when no priest is available, the celebrant or deacon, and other communicants, reverently eat and drink it, either after the Communion of the people or after the Dismissal.
A hymn may be sung before or after the postcommunion prayer.

NEW ZEALAND 1989
A New Zealand Prayer Book (Collins, Auckland and London, 1989), includes 'A Service of the Word with Holy Communion' (pp 518-520). The first extract is the prayers of thanksgiving and the second is an optional prayer that may follow the peace.

TEXT 8
Then follow The Prayers of the People, not including The Lord's Prayer.
This prayer follows

Let us give glory to God, our Creator, Redeemer and Sanctifier.
Glory to God in the highest.
Glory to God in the highest.

God our Creator, we thank you for the world you have made; we thank you for your loving care watching over all creation; we thank you for entrusting part of your world to us to tend, to care for and to develop.
Glory to God in the highest.

You have made us, women and men in your image, so that in each other we can trace your likeness and serve you by serving our brother and sisters.
Glory to God in the highest.

You made us to know you and to be near you, our hearts are restless until we come to you. To bring us nearer to you when we were still far off, you sent your prophets and teachers to show us the glory of your steadfast love.
Glory to God in the highest.

The wonder of your redeeming love was fully shown in Jesus the Christ, who walked among us as one of us, meeting us face to face, person to person, God in human form.
Glory to God in the highest.

Yet we did not value him and sent him to death, a death he freely accepted, stretching out his arms on the cross to embrace the whole human race and to bear our sin in himself.
By his death and resurrection, death is destroyed and we are delivered from sin to share his risen life.
Glory to God in the highest.

You sent your Holy Spirit upon your Church so that, in Jesus, we are united to you, Father, with all the redeemed.
Glory to God in the highest.

We thank you that we can worship you with prayer and praise as one with all your people. Above all we thank you for this sacrament and the body and blood of Christ.
Glory to God in the highest.

TEXT 9
The minister may continue
God, creator of time and space, may the love and faith which makes this bread the body of Christ this wine his blood enfold us now. Make us one with (the people of . . .* and) the whole body of Christ. May Christ's Holy Spirit bring to us in the sacrament the strength we need, and an abiding trust in your gift of eternal life. **Amen.**

WALES 1974
This text on the next page is that agreed by the bench of Bishops in the Church in Wales April 1974. It provides directions based on the eucharistic rite.

TEXT 10
Order for public administration of Holy Communion from the Reserved
Sacrament by a Deacon.

By permission of the bishop in cases of pastoral emergency.

1. *Preparation and Ministry of the Word, with the substitution of the Collect for
   Trinity XXI for the Absolution, to the end of the Intercession.*

   In place of the Ministry of the Sacrament:

2. Let us pray

   Blessed Lord, who in a wonderful Sacrament hast left us a memorial of
   thy Passion: Grant us, we beseech thee, so to venerate the sacred mysteries of thy Body and Blood, that we may ever perceive within ourselves the fruit of thy redemption, who livest and reignest with the
   Father and the Holy Ghost, one God, world without end. Amen.

   Act of Recollection
   We come with the whole family of God to obey our Lord's command
   and to link our act of worship with that of all God's people in the whole
   Church as they offer the Eucharist of His Body and Blood.
   We become one in Christ.

3. *The Prayer of Humble Access may be used.*
4. *The Lord's Prayer . . .*

SCOTLAND 1992
The General Synod of the Scottish Episcopal Church published *Communion* in
1992. This is directions for 'The Administration of Holy Communion from the
Reserved Sacrament (when the minister is a deacon or lay person)'. The first
extract is the prayer said after 'the Service of the Word' once the consecrated
elements are place on the altar. This thanksgiving prayer is one of three (the third
being the General Thanksgiving) said in the midst of the congregation before the
Agnus Dei. It is 'from the Deacon's Proclamation Liturgy of Addai and Mari'
(p.4).

TEXT 11
Standing at the altar, the minister says:
'We remember in prayer those who celebrated the eucharist at . . . ' *(here
naming the congregation and the service at which the elements were consecrated),*
'with whom we now share in communion through this consecrated bread
and wine . . .'

TEXT 12
First Thanksgiving Prayer
God of all love we draw near with awe and reverence to the mystery of our
Saviour's Body and Blood.
R. **Lord have mercy**

May we commemorate his passion and recall his resurrection with pure
hearts and unclouded faith.
R. **Lord have mercy**

For our sake he took body and soul, human, mortal, tried and tempted as we
are, and by his preaching of the kingdom called us to the knowledge of your
truth.
R. **Lord have mercy**

When he had fulfilled all your mind he was lifted up upon the cross, and
rose from the dead, and was taken up into heaven to be the first-fruits of our
human nature, the author and perfecter of faith.
R. **Lord have mercy**

Now he calls us to his table to become partakers of his grace.
R. **Lord have mercy**

With a humble will and with overflowing love may we receive your gift of
everlasting life.
R. **Lord have mercy**

With pure prayer and abundant hope may we leave with you those things
that are past and devote ourselves afresh to your service.
R. **Lord have mercy**

Grant us to receive the Holy One and to be hallowed by the Holy Spirit.
Amen.

Grant us to share in the peace of Christ through the sacrament of peace.
Amen.

May this holy communion bring us to new life in your kingdom and unite
us with all your Saints. **Amen.**

RELIGIOUS (nd)
Religious communities may lack priests. The following is a text authorized by
the bishop for a women's Religious Community, and is based on the English
ASB Rite A.

TEXT 13
*(At this time the deaconess reverently takes the consecrated Sacrament from the aumbry
and places a sufficient number of hosts in a ciborium (or on a paten) which is resting on
a corporal.)*

Deaconess The Lord is here.
All   **His Spirit is with us.**
D   Lift up your hearts.
All   **We lift them to the Lord.**
D   Let us give thanks to the Lord our God.
All   **It is right to give him thanks and praise.**
D   It is indeed right, . . . [as in Rite A, First Eucharistic Prayer] . . . made us
a people for your own possession.
(Proper preface, when appropriate, S.76)
D   Therefore with angels and archangels . . .
All   **Holy, holy . . .**
D   We thank you heavenly Father for the institution and celebration of
the Holy Eucharist. We join ourselves to the previous celebrations at
this altar and throughout the world at this time. As we eat these
previously consecrated gifts in the presence of your divine majesty,
renew us by your Spirit, inspire us with your love, and unite us in the
body of your Son, Jesus Christ our Lord.
Through him, and with him, and in him . . .
All   **Blessing and honour and glory . . .**

ENGLAND 1983
Ministry to the Sick (University Press, Oxford, 1983) includes a rite for 'The
Distribution of Communion to those not present at a Celebration'. In it 'the
minister explains this ministry of communion using the following or other
suitable words' (p.21 §10).

TEXT 14
The Church of God, of which we are members, had taken bread and wine
and given thanks over them according to our Lord's command. I bring these
holy gifts that you may share in the communion of his body and blood. We
who are many are one body, because we all share in one bread.

Alcuin/GROW Joint Liturgical Studies

All cost £3.95 (US $8) in 1993 and 1994

1987 TITLES

1988 TITLES

1989 TITLES

1990 TITLES

1991 TITLES

1992 TITLES

1993 TITLES

1994 TITLES (exact wording not yet final)